A NEW APPROACH
St Mark's Gospel

A NEW APPROACH

St Mark's Gospel

Michael Wilcockson

Hodder Murray

A MEMBER OF THE HODDER HEADLINE GROUP

This book is dedicated to Chris Morley who first introduced me to Mark's Gospel.

Quotations from the Bible are from the New International Version. Examination boards do not specify which version should be used, although you should be familiar with the titles they give to the set passages from Mark's Gospel.

This book uses the usual BCE and CE to refer to dates. BCE means Before the Common Era and is equivalent to BC (Before Christ). CE means Common Era and is equivalent to AD (Anno Domini) or the time after Jesus' birth.

This book refers to the first part of the Bible as the **Old Testament**, because for most Christians it is seen as a preparation for Jesus. However, a lot of people today call it the **Hebrew Bible** not only out of respect for Jews, for whom it is not a preparation for the coming of Jesus, but because they feel this is not the right way to read it.

The Publishers would like to thank the following for permission to reproduce copyright material:
AKG Images: pp. 35 (top) (engraving by F Olivier), 43, 52, 58, 104, 111; AKG Images/ Brueghel: p. 26; AKG Images/ Cameraphoto: p. 102 (middle left); AKG Images/ Alexei von Jawlensky: p. 102 (bottom left); AKG Images/ Erich Lessing: pp. 5, 102 (top right and bottom middle); AKG Images/ Pirozzi: p. 107; AKG Images/ Rabatti – Dominigie: p. 102 (top middle); Ancient Art and Architecture Collection: pp. 1 and 3; BDI Images Ltd: p. 30 (right); © Bettmann/ CORBIS: p. 74; The Bible Society, *Jesus of Nazareth*: pp. 19, 38, 41, 47, 51, 69, 71, 80, 81 (top and bottom), 86, 88, 90, 106; CAIN (http://cain.ulst.ac.uk/photographs/): p. 49; Church House Publishing for the cover image of *Issues in Human Sexuality: A Statement by the House of Bishops*: p. 67 (right); Circa Photo Library: p. 102 (centre top); Circa Photo Library/ © John Smith: pp. 11, 20, 21, 76, 82; Circa Photo Library/ © Barrie Searle: pp. 66, 67 (left); © Richard Cummings/ CORBIS: p. 31 (right); Echternach Gospels Lectionary Bibliotheque Royale Albert 1er, Brussells: p. 102 (centre bottom); Edifice: p. 29; © Luis Galdamez/ Reuters/ Corbis: p. 99; Getty Images: p. 105; © Louise Gubb/ CORBIS SABA: p. 113; © Chris Hellier/ CORBIS: p. 35 (bottom) (engraving of Jesus Walking on Water by Dore, 1866); © Historical Picture Archive/ CORBIS: p. 57; courtesy of Hodder archive, reproduced courtesy of the Director and University Librarian, The John Rylands University Library of Manchester: p. 8; © Hulton-Deutsch Collection / CORBIS: p. 6; LJA130256 Kwerata Reesu, 1994 (by Laura James) Private Collection/ Bridgeman Art Library: p. 102 (middle right); © Alain Nogues/ COR-BIS SYGMA: p. 102 (bottom right); © Richard T. Nowitz/ CORBIS: p. 73; PA PHOTOS/ EPA: p. 17; © Steve Raymer/ Corbis: p. 62 (left); © Reuters/ CORBIS: p. 53; courtesy of © Benjamin Rondel/ CORBIS: p. 63; © Royalty-free/ CORBIS: pp. 18, 31 (left), 55, 62 (right); © Ted Spiegel/ Corbis: p. 30 (left); Still Pictures/ Glen Christian: p. 27; © Les Stone/ CORBIS: p. 102 (top left); Michael Wilcockson: pp. 28, 68, 91, 110; World Religious Photo Library, JULL14A8: p. 108.

Everymans Library Classics for the extract from the Athanasian Creed taken from *The Book of Common Prayer* (1999); Fount for the extract from *Miracles* by C S Lewis (1998); Marshall, Morgan & Scott, London for the extract from *The Gospel of Mark* by Hugh Anderson (1976); Oxford: Lion Publishing for the extract from *A Guide to Science and Belief* by Michael Poole (1997, 2nd Edition); SCM, London for the extract from *Miracles In Dispute* by E and M-L Keller (1969).

Scripture quotations taken from the HOLY BIBLE, NEW INTERNATIONAL VERSION.
Copyright © 1973, 1978, 1984 by International Bible Society.
Used by permission of Hodder & Stoughton Publishers,
A member of the Hodder Headline Group.
All rights reserved.
"NIV" is a registered trademark of International Bible Society.
UK trademark number 1448790.

All artwork by Barking Dog Art.

Every effort has been made to trace all copyright holders, but if any have been inadvertently overlooked the Publishers will be pleased to make the necessary arrangements at the first opportunity.

Although every effort has been made to ensure that website addresses are correct at time of going to press, Hodder Murray cannot be held responsible for the content of any website mentioned in this book. It is sometimes possible to find a relocated web page by typing in the address of the home page for a website in the URL window of your browser.

Orders: please contact Bookpoint Ltd, 130 Milton Park, Abingdon, Oxon OX14 4SB. Telephone: (44) 01235 827720.
Fax: (44) 01235 400454. Lines are open from 9.00–5.00, Monday to Saturday, with a 24-hour message answering service.
Visit our website at www.hoddereducation.co.uk.

© Michael Wilcockson 2005
First published in 2005 by
Hodder Murray, a member of the Hodder Headline Group
338 Euston Road
London NW1 3BH

Impression number   10 9 8 7 6 5 4 3 2
Year   2010 2009 2008 2007 2006

Cover photo courtesy of Wolfgang Kaehler/CORBIS.
Typeset in 10.5 on 13pt Berling by Phoenix Photosetting, Lordswood, Chatham, Kent
Printed in Dubai

A catalogue record for this title is available from the British Library
ISBN-10: 0 340 81465 9
ISBN-13: 978 0 340 81465 9

Contents

UNIT ONE | Gospel and Authority

1

KEY WORDS

Conservatives: Those who believe that the Bible is true but may contain human interpretations.

Eyewitnesses: Those who saw and heard what Jesus did and said.

Fundamentalists: Those who consider that the Bible is God's Word and therefore cannot be in error.

Gospel: The good news that Jesus is God's Son.

Liberals: Those who believe that the Bible is written by humans in their own words.

Literalists: Those who consider every word of the Bible is God-given.

New Testament: is the second part of the Christian Bible, which proclaims that Jesus is the Son of God.

Old Testament: is the Jewish Hebrew Bible and for Christians the preparation for the New Testament.

Word of God: The way in which God expresses himself to humans.

Word-of-mouth: Describes the stories and sayings of Jesus, as they were passed on orally. Referred to by scholars as the oral tradition.

KEY QUESTION

What are the gospels and why were they written?

WHAT IS 'GOSPEL'?

The word **gospel** is derived from the Greek word *euangelion*. Its basic meaning is 'good news', and it often appears in the **New Testament**, especially in Paul's letters. In Christian terms it refers to the good news that the promised messiah has come and has lived, died and risen in order to bring salvation to the world. This is the gospel that the first Christians believed and preached. It can be summarised in the simple phrase 'Jesus is the Christ'. So the first Christians were those Jews who heard the gospel, and believed that Jesus was the fulfilment of **Old Testament** prophecy. This is what divided the very early Christians from the rest of the Jews. Under the leadership of Saint Paul, the apostles preached the gospel to the Gentiles of the Greek/Roman world. The Gentiles proved much more responsive to this new preaching than the Jews had been. They could see the spiritual and moral results of the gospel and were less bothered by the theological problems that worried the Jews.

This coin from the reign of Herod the Great reminds us that Jesus was teaching during the time when the Romans controlled Palestine.

WHY WERE THE GOSPELS WRITTEN?

When the word gospel is used in the New Testament it refers not to a text or a book but to a spoken message. The verbs used with it are never verbs such as 'write' or 'read', but 'announce', 'proclaim', 'speak' or 'hear'. So when it became a title describing a certain kind of book, the word gospel was being put to a new use – and the result was a very new kind of writing. The gospel is not neutral but wants to *persuade* the reader to see the truth of what it is presenting.

When were the gospels written?

We do not know exactly when the gospels were written, but we can work out approximate dates based on the historical events of the time.

- The Roman general Pompey conquered Jerusalem in 63 BCE and later, in 37 BCE, placed Palestine under direct Roman control by making the half-Jew Herod the Great (37–4 BCE) king.
- Jesus was born around 4 BCE. Recent historians consider that earlier scholars have miscalculated the time of Jesus' birth.
- When Herod the Great died in 4 BCE his kingdom was divided up between his three sons. Archelaus, who was given Judea (the southern territory) to rule, turned out to be a very bad ruler and was removed by the Romans. Eventually, Pontius Pilate was appointed procurator or governor. He governed from 26–36 CE.
- Jesus was sentenced to death and crucified in 29 or 30 CE aged 33 years old.

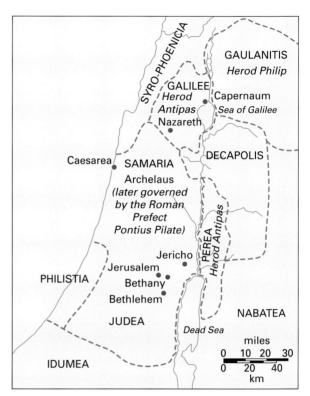

Palestine in the first century CE.

Here is how Mark and Luke open their gospels. Read these passages and write down what you think each writer says the gospel is all about.

The beginning of the gospel about Jesus Christ, the Son of God ... After John was put in prison, Jesus went into Galilee, proclaiming the good news of God. 'The time has come,' he said. 'The Kingdom of God is near. Repent and believe the good news!'

Mark 1:1 and 1:14–15

Many have undertaken to draw up an account of the things that have been fulfilled among us, just as they were handed down to us by those who from the first were eyewitnesses and servants of the Word. Therefore, since I myself have carefully investigated everything from the beginning, it seemed good also to me to write an orderly account for you, most excellent Theophilus, so that you may know the certainty of the things you have been taught.

Luke 1:1–4

Inscription from Caesarea (the place where Pilate resided), recording 'Pontius Pilate, Prefect of Judea'. This is the first recorded mention of Pilate outside the gospels. It was Pilate who gave the order that Jesus should be crucified.

This picture is based on some of the detail of Titus' arch in Rome. It shows the Roman soldiers removing some of the sacred Temple treasures after the fall of Jerusalem in 70 CE.

- Christianity spread fast after Jesus' death beyond Israel and throughout the Mediterranean world, being preached by people such as St Paul.

- A major fire in Rome during the Emperor Nero's reign in 64 CE was blamed on the Christians living there. Nero carried out some terrible tortures and punishments on the Christians. It is probable that the fire was started by Nero himself. According to tradition, Paul and Peter died as martyrs during these persecutions.

- Increasingly during this period, little groups of militant Jews called the Zealots were dissatisfied with their Jewish leaders and Roman rulers. Open revolt began in 66 CE and came to a climax in 70 CE when the Temple in Jerusalem was destroyed by the Romans as they put down the revolution.

Mark's Gospel could have been written shortly after 30 CE. But to begin with, as the gospel was to be preached, the stories and sayings about Jesus were passed on by **word-of-mouth**. The gospel would have been carefully learnt. This is referred to by scholars as the oral tradition – that is, the period before Jesus' teaching and life were written down. An example of the oral tradition can be found in St Paul's letter to the

Corinthians where St Paul tells us that the gospel he first heard and then passed on contained the main teaching of Jesus, his crucifixion and resurrection.

> For what I received I passed on to you as of the first importance: that Christ died for our sins according to the Scriptures, that he was buried, that he was raised on the third day according to the Scriptures, and that he appeared to Peter and then to the Twelve.

1 Corinthians 15:3–5 (52–55 CE)

So it is unlikely that Mark's Gospel was written as early as 30 CE. It is more likely that Mark wrote his gospel between 64 and 70 CE, because various hints in the text reflect the times of fear and uncertainty.

■ Mark's Gospel has a strong sense of urgency about it. He frequently uses the words 'and then' and 'straight away' and 'immediately'. Perhaps he thinks that the disasters in society mark the beginning of the end of the world when God would judge the world, and that consequently the gospel must be preached as quickly as possible.

■ The setting of Mark 13 suggests a time of persecution when members of families will betray each other, but it also encourages the Christian community to be strong. The gospel

TASK BOX

a) When do you think Mark wrote his gospel? Give your reasons.

b) Explain the reasons why Mark wrote down the gospel rather than continue to pass it on by word of mouth.

c) What would Mark's purpose be in writing a gospel if he was writing during a time of persecution?

is very critical of the Jewish authorities. Mark collects together a series of debates with the leaders of Judaism – the Sadducees, chief priests, lawyers and senior Pharisees (Mark 12) – which reflect the tensions between ordinary people and leading Jews.

Most scholars consider that Matthew, Luke and John wrote after Mark. The situation revealed in these gospels is less tense than in Mark and suggests a time of writing after 70 CE.

WHO WROTE MARK'S GOSPEL?

None of the gospel writers identify themselves by stating their own name. The names Matthew, Mark, Luke and John were attached to the texts at a later stage. However, they were not simply chosen at random. There is good reason to think that Mark did indeed compile the gospel which bears his name, because Papias, the bishop of Hierapolis (130–140 CE), wrote that he had found out that Mark was Peter's 'interpreter' or secretary.

> Mark, having been the interpreter of Peter, wrote down accurately all that Peter mentioned, whether sayings or doings of Christ; not, however, in order.

Bishop Papias (60–130 CE)

There are some good reasons for considering that a person called Luke really did write Luke's Gospel. There seem to be clear links between the apostle John and the gospel which bears his name. Matthew, however, is more of a puzzle. He may well be 'Matthew' the tax collector, whose call to discipleship is recorded in the Gospel of Matthew (even though Mark's Gospel calls him 'Levi').

Can we know who Mark actually was?

■ Many think Mark was the same John Mark who is recorded in Acts of the Apostles as accompanying Paul on his first missionary journey (Acts 12:12, 13:1–5). Mark appears to have had his home in Jerusalem and to have mixed with the first apostles.

- At one stage he and Paul appear to have had an argument and Mark was sent away (Acts 15:37–40), but later they seem to have made up their differences and Paul mentions him in his later letters.

 Get Mark and bring him with you, because he is helpful to me in my ministry.

2 Timothy 4:11

Paul's request in his letter to Timothy.

- Bishop Papias linked Mark with Peter, and in one of Peter's letters he calls Mark his 'son' or pupil.
- Mark is a fairly common name in the first century and we cannot be certain whether the John Mark in Acts is necessarily the same Mark who wrote the gospel.
- Even though John Mark may have lived in Jerusalem, his gospel doesn't demonstrate a good knowledge of the city (as John's Gospel does), and often appears to have a confused knowledge of other places in Galilee and Judea.
- On the other hand, Peter is a central figure in Mark's Gospel, and (even though he is not always portrayed in a particularly good light) it is possible that Mark had access to material from Peter.

Where did Mark write?

- Many suggest that Mark was writing in Rome during the time of Nero's persecution of the early Christians. These were the years before and after the great fire in Rome in 64 CE, which many believed had been started by Nero and which he and others blamed on the Christians.
- Mark explains quite a few Jewish customs that perhaps only Palestinian Jews carried out, so he may have been writing for Jewish converts or Roman/Greek converts outside Palestine.

- But Mark could have written his gospel in any major town in the Mediterranean world where there was a mix of Jews, Greeks and Romans.

A statue of the Emperor Nero in Rome. Nero persecuted the early Christians.

 When you see 'the abomination that causes desolation' standing where it does not belong – let the reader understand – then let those who are in Judea flee to the mountains.

Mark 13:14

It is possible that this strange passage may be a reference to the Emperor Nero as the 'abomination'; the one who was hated and feared because of his evil behaviour.

TEST YOURSELF

1 Who was Papias and what did he say about Mark's Gospel?
2 Where did John Mark live?
3 What was Mark's association with Paul?
4 What happened in Rome in 64 CE?
5 Give one reason why Mark might have written his gospel in Rome.

Did Mark write to encourage Christians during persecution?

The historian Tacitus (55–120 CE) recorded how the early Christians were horribly tortured and killed in Rome in the year 64 CE. There is good evidence, as we have seen, that Mark wrote to give early Christians encouragement during these times.

> Accordingly, an arrest was first made of all who pleaded guilty; then, upon their information, an immense multitude was convicted, not so much of the crime of firing the city, as of hatred against mankind. Mockery of every sort was added to their deaths. Covered with the skins of beasts, they were torn by dogs and perished, or were nailed to crosses, or were doomed to the flames and burnt, to serve as a nightly illumination when daylight had expired. Nero offered his gardens for the spectacle, and was exhibiting a show in the circus, while he mingled with the people in the dress of a charioteer.
>
> *Tacitus* Annals *XV*

Many think that Mark 13, which is sometimes called the Little Apocalypse, reflects a time of great tension and worry. It describes a period of wars, family break-ups and persecution. Mark records Jesus' words so that those who have been arrested and are being tried by the law courts are encouraged not to worry but to trust the guidance of the Holy Spirit (13:10–11). Those who 'stand firm' and keep the faith will be saved (13:13).

> Brother will betray brother to death, and a father his child. Children will rebel against their parents and have them put to death. All men will hate you because of me, but he who stands firm to the end will be saved.
>
> *Mark 13:12–13*

The same advice is given, for example, in the Parable of the Sower (4:1–8) when Jesus talks of those whose faith has 'no root' or is unable to sustain itself in difficult times. In his explanation (4:17) Jesus says that these times might include persecutions. It is possible that Mark has added this word to reflect the times in which he lived.

The effect of the atomic bomb at Hiroshima. Many think that nuclear war will be like the apocalyptic end that Jesus talks about in Mark 13, 'the sun will be darkened, and the moon will not give its light; the stars will fall from the sky, and the heavenly bodies will be shaken.' (Mark 13:24–28) How do you think the world will end?

A New Approach – St Mark's Gospel

Throughout the gospel the disciples frequently fail to live up to Jesus' teaching. For example, Peter falls asleep just before Jesus' own arrest and trial in the Garden of Gethsemane. Jesus says to him, 'Could you not keep watch for one hour?' (14:37). Being awake and alert is the theme of Mark 13 and Mark would have understood that the 'hour' is the crucial time of testing during persecution and suffering.

Another important story for Mark that illustrates a time of persecution is when Jesus predicts the death and martyrdom of two of his own closest disciples: James and John (10:38). Jesus says they will drink the same 'cup' as Jesus will; that is, the cup of suffering and death. It is probable that by the time Mark wrote about this he knew they had died as martyrs. James was put to death by Herod Agrippa I in 44 CE (Acts 12:1–5). But Mark may just have wanted to use the example of James and John to make a more general point. Just before this prediction, Jesus had taught that all those who suffered the loss of family and home for their faith and persecutions (10:29–31) would be rewarded with eternal life after death.

On the other hand, Mark may not have been writing during a particular period of official persecution carried out by the Romans or Jews. He may just have been giving general encouragement to all those who had become Christians and were suffering for their faith as a result.

TEST YOURSELF

1 What did the historian Tacitus write about the persecution of Christians by Nero?
2 What is the 'Little Apocalypse'?
3 Who will guide Christians when they are persecuted?
4 In which year was James put to death?

TASK BOX

a) Read Mark 14:43–15:37. Christians believe that they should follow the example of Jesus. From this passage give examples of the way in which Jesus:
- kept to his principles
- showed courage and faith
- endured physical pain
- did not retaliate
- showed compassion
- showed humility
- showed his trust in God
- showed forgiveness.

b) Read Mark 4:1–20 and Unit 3 (page 27), Mark 8:34–38 and Unit 5 (page 53). Explain what these passages teach a Christian about how to behave under persecution.

c) Recently, statues have been placed in Westminster Abbey to commemorate the deaths of the following Christians who have died as a result of their faith: The Grand Duchess Elizabeth, Manche Masemola, Maximilian Kobe, Lucian Tapiedi, Dietrich Bonhoeffer, Esther John, Wang Zhiming, Janani Luwum and Oscar Romero.

Find out about **one** of them. Describe and explain how this person lived their life according to the gospel.

You can go to the following website and use the 'Quick Search' facility: www.westminster-abbey.org

Where did Mark get his material from?

- We have already suggested that Mark was not an **eyewitness**, although one small detail refers to a young man running away naked at Jesus' arrest. Some argue that this might have been Mark's way of saying that he was there (Mark 14:51–52).

- Some sections, such as Mark 13, the Little Apocalypse, probably existed as a separate document before Mark found it and inserted it into his gospel.

- Papias says that Mark wrote down things 'not in order'. Many scholars note how Mark's style is very uneven and his paragraphs are short. This may suggest that he was writing down the gospel in the way that it had been remembered and passed on by word-of-mouth. Mark has not done much more than fit the stories together like a string of beads on a necklace.

- He may have translated these word-of-mouth sayings from Aramaic (a type of Hebrew) into basic Greek. This suggests that some of the material was received straight from Peter and other early followers.

- But Mark is a skilled writer and has developed his own themes and ideas. This is clearer when the gospels are compared to each other.

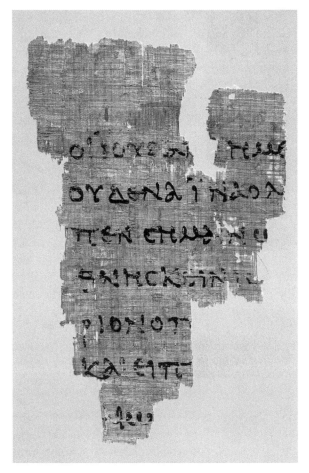

A very early manuscript fragment of the New Testament written in the original Greek language.

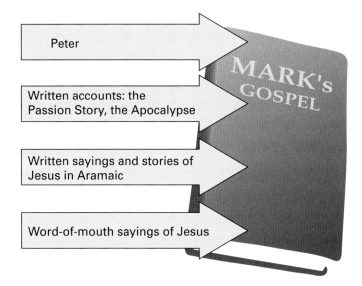

The possible sources for Mark's Gospel. How important do you think Peter was for Mark?

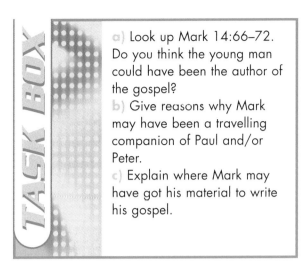
copied, making the text much shorter as a pocket-book version. Many today argue that in fact Mark is the earliest gospel, and was copied and modified by Matthew and Luke. But the debate continues and there are many who support the view that Matthew wrote first. As the gospels of Matthew, Mark and Luke have a very similar order and style they are called the synoptic gospels – 'synoptic' in Greek means to 'see together' – because they see the events in a similar way. John's Gospel gives a more abstract presentation of Jesus and it is much more difficult to know whether he had come across the other gospels.

WHY ARE THERE FOUR GOSPELS?

KEY QUESTION

Why are there four gospels and not just one?

An important question is why there are four gospels. A traditional answer might be that each of the writers was there with Jesus and wrote down what he saw. This would account for some of the differences. But when we read many passages side by side we immediately notice that word order, use of vocabulary, grammar and other details are included in such a way that suggests that the purpose of some of the writers was to copy and adapt one or more of the other gospels.

The question is, therefore, who was copying from whom?

For a long time Church scholars argued that Matthew was the oldest gospel and that Mark

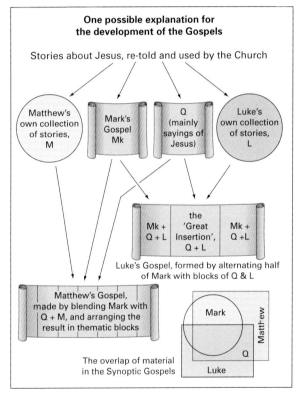

One possible explanation for the development of the Gospels

Stories about Jesus, re-told and used by the Church

Matthew's own collection of stories, M

Mark's Gospel Mk

Q (mainly sayings of Jesus)

Luke's own collection of stories, L

Mk + Q + L | the 'Great Insertion', Q + L | Mk + Q +L

Luke's Gospel, formed by alternating half of Mark with blocks of Q & L

Matthew's Gospel, made by blending Mark with Q + M, and arranging the result in thematic blocks

The overlap of material in the Synoptic Gospels

Mark

Matthew

Q

Luke

The relationship of the three synoptic gospels.

Read these four accounts of Jesus' Cleansing of the Temple.

a) Make a list of the details each gospel writer shares with the others.
b) Make a list of the details that are different.
c) Do you think all four are eyewitness accounts?
d) Is one of these accounts the basis for the others? If so, which one?
e) 'The Church should have only put one gospel in the New Testament.'
Do you agree? Give reasons for your answer.

Mark 11:15-18	Matthew 21:12-13	Luke 19:45-48	John 2:13-17
15 On reaching Jerusalem, Jesus entered the Temple area and began driving out those who were buying and selling there. He overturned the tables of the money-changers and the benches of those selling doves, 16 and would not allow anyone to carry merchandise through the Temple courts. 17 And as he taught them, he said, 'Is it not written: "My house will be called a house of prayer for all nations"? But you have made it "a den of robbers".' 18 The chief priests and the teachers of the law heard this and began looking for a way to kill him, for they feared him, because the whole crowd was amazed at his teaching.	12 Jesus entered the Temple area and drove out all who were buying and selling there. He overturned the tables of the money-changers and the benches of those selling doves. 13 'It is written,' he said to them, '"My house will be called a house of prayer", but you are making it a "den of robbers".'	45 Then he entered the Temple area and began driving out those who were selling. 46 'It is written,' he said to them, '"My house will be a house of prayer"; but you have made it "a den of robbers".' 47 Every day he was teaching at the Temple. But the chief priests, the teachers of the law and the leaders among the people were trying to kill him. 48 Yet they could not find any way to do it, because all the people hung on his words.	13 When it was almost time for the Jewish Passover, Jesus went up to Jerusalem. 14 In the Temple courts he found men selling cattle, sheep and doves, and others sitting at tables exchanging money. 15 So he made a whip out of cords, and drove all from the Temple area, both sheep and cattle; he scattered the coins of the money-changers and overturned their tables. 16 To those who sold doves he said, 'Get these out of here! How dare you turn my Father's house into a market!' 17 His disciples remembered that it is written: 'Zeal for your house will consume me.'

KEY QUESTION

Why do different Christians today interpret the gospels in such different ways?

The gospels are especially important for Christians today because they give an account of Jesus' life and teaching, which they can continue to study and discuss for meaning and relevance. The gospels are therefore said to have authority because they are considered to be a foundation for Christian belief. But Christians differ in the way they understand the authority of the text, and therefore also differ in the way in which it should be interpreted. This is a complex issue.

Literalists consider that, as the writers were inspired by God's Holy Spirit to compose their gospels, every word is the **Word of God**. Literalists often quote St Paul's remark to Timothy that all scripture, that is the whole Bible, is inspired directly by God.

 All scripture is given by inspiration of God.

2 Timothy 3:16

For many Christians the Bible is the Word of God and is very significant for living a good life.

Fundamentalists also believe that the gospels are the Word of God and are 'fundamental' to Christian belief. Some fundamentalists are literalists, but most argue that different parts of the gospels have to be interpreted in different ways. Some passages are intended to be taken literally and some as metaphors or symbols. For example, when Jesus says that if your hand causes you sin it should be cut off (Mark 9:43) he means you look for the cause off that sin and put it right. He doesn't mean literally that a Christian should chop off his hand, because that wouldn't solve the fundamental problem of the sin. There are no contradictions in the gospels, and if there appear to be, then it is likely that one passage is to be read literally and the other as a metaphor. Fundamentalists consider that miracles cannot be disproved by modern science because they are examples of the power of God working through his Son, Jesus Christ.

Make sure you include all these things and they mean this...but you can put it in your own words.

God created the world in seven days, that is seven periods of time.

Conservatives also consider that the gospels are inspired but that they are, nevertheless, written by humans who have their own ways of seeing and interpreting things and who sometimes include their own details. There may well be contradictions between the gospels, but what matters is the deeper meaning. For example, the resurrection stories in all four gospels vary quite considerably but none disagree on the basic idea of the resurrection.

Liberals consider that each writer was inspired to compose their gospel much in the same way that a great novelist or poet writes. This allows each writer much more freedom to express himself according to his own experience of God and the needs of those reading or listening to his gospel. Liberals argue that when we interpret the gospels today we have to take into account the fact that we are dealing with ancient texts written in very different times from our own. For example, many people today don't think that the world is a battleground between evil forces in the underworld and good forces in the sky – but that was the view of the first century. Liberals argue that we should interpret these ideas as metaphors or symbols of the uncertainties of life. Evil spirits should be re-expressed psychologically as our deep-seated fears and anxieties about life.

How can I put this symbolically?

PERSPECTIVES

Interpreting the story of Legion today

How might Christians today interpret the story of the curing of Mob or Legion (Mark 5:1–20)? In the story, Mark tells how Legion – the man who is possessed by many evil spirits – has been chained up outside a village because he frightens the villagers by screaming and cutting himself. When Jesus visits him the evil spirits recognise him and beg him to send them into a herd of pigs nearby. When Jesus does this, the pigs stampede over the edge of the hill and are drowned. Legion is now cured but the locals are terrified and ask Jesus to leave. Jesus sends the cured man back to his family to tell them what God has done for him.

- As a **literalist** I think Legion or Mob's illness was due to his possession by many evil spirits. I don't think modern science is right to say that he was just psychologically disturbed. I believe this story shows the power of Jesus as God's Son to expel these very powerful demons out of Legion into the pigs. Christianity is about the triumph of good over evil.

- I agree with everything my literalist friend has said, but as a **fundamentalist** I think she has to explain why, for example, in Matthew's account (Matthew 8:28) there are *two* demon-filled men. I think it is more than likely that there would have been more than one person rejected by the villagers because of their violent and frightening behaviour. This just shows what happens to a society that lacks faith in God and in Jesus Christ to challenge evil. The fundamental message is that only God can change society, which is why Jesus sends Legion back to his family to preach the good news.

- As a **conservative** I think we must remember that when Mark wrote during times of persecution the threat of evil was very real and frightening. That is why he has exaggerated aspects of the story to show that evil – however powerful – will be overcome by God. Mark has therefore exaggerated the speed of the man's sudden, complete mental and physical cure. Perhaps he has added the story of the pigs to show just how effective the cure was.

- The trouble with all the views expressed so far is that all assume evil is a separate power. As a **liberal Christian** I think we should focus on the story of hope which belief in God brings. The man's possession by demons is a way of talking about his mental illness or his own sense of despair by being rejected by society. I think we should interpret the movement of the evil spirits from the man into the pigs as a symbol of his old life disappearing and his new life of peace and happiness beginning.

Discuss which of the four types of interpretation you agree with most and which you find least satisfactory.

TASK BOX

Read the following sayings of Jesus.

- If anyone would come after me, he must deny himself and take up his cross and follow me ... *(8:34)*
- And if your eye causes you to sin, pluck it out ... *(9:47)*
- Anyone who divorces his wife and marries another woman commits adultery against her ... *(10:11)*

Discuss whether they should be interpreted literally or metaphorically or both.

1 a. (i) Describe the persecution of Christians in Rome by Nero.

(ii) Explain why some people think Mark's Gospel was written for non-Jews facing persecution.

(iii) Explain how the example of Jesus might help Christians facing persecution today. [12]

b. 'Christians today are not prepared to suffer as Jesus did.'

Do you agree? Give reasons for your opinion, showing you have considered another point of view. In your answer you should refer to Mark's Gospel. [8]

2 'It's really important that Peter was in the room when Jesus healed Jairus' daughter and that he told Mark what happened. That way we can be sure all the details are true. Why, we even know the girl's age!' Ben

'I don't agree with you. I don't think we need to know exactly what happened.' Stephanie

a. Give **two** other details from Mark's story about Jairus' daughter that Ben might have mentioned. [4]

b. Give **two** sources of authority other than Peter that Mark might have used for his gospel. [4]

c. Explain why Christians like Stephanie disagree with Ben's viewpoint. [7]

d. 'Mark's Gospel was written almost 2000 years ago, so it cannot mean anything for people today.'

Do you agree? Give reasons for your answer, showing that you have thought about more than one point of view. [5]

Assignment

WEBLINKS

- For looking up Bible references: http://bible.gospelcom.net/bible
- Nero and the fire of Rome: www.bible-history.com/nero/index.html
- Christian martyrs at Westminster Abbey: www.westminster-abbey.org/
- The Chicago statement in full: www.iclnet.org/pub/resources/text/history/chicago.stm
- On the synoptic problem: www.ntgateway.com/synoptic/

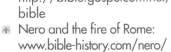

REMEMBER

- Mark was probably the first gospel to be written.
- Mark wrote about 40 years after Jesus' death.
- Mark's Gospel gives encouragement to those suffering persecution for their faith.
- Some modern Christians consider that Mark has recorded Jesus' words exactly as he said them.
- Some modern Christians think Mark has interpreted Jesus' teachings according to his own situation.

2

KEY WORDS

The age to come: In Jewish thought many of the prophets looked forward to a time when God would remove all suffering and injustice. They contrasted the age to come with the present age, the times in which we still live.

Baptism: The moment when, for many Christians, a person becomes a member of the Christian Church (or worldwide community of Christians).

Eschatology: The technical word used to mean discussion of the future when God will establish a new and perfect world.

Repentance: Repentance is more than just saying sorry; it is a change of heart and mind, leading to a new way of life.

KEY QUESTION

What would a perfect world be like?
Can humans achieve it by themselves?

THE COMING OF THE KINGDOM OF GOD

A very basic human desire is for a better world. For some, a better world can be achieved through force or revolution; for some, it is a slow process of political reforms; for others, it is only possible if God acts in the world.

In the Old Testament many of the prophets looked forward to a better world. Isaiah, for example, describes this as a time when all suffering would be removed and the blind would see and the deaf would be able to hear (Isaiah 35:5–6). He also describes a time when God's glory or presence will be experienced by everyone in the world (Isaiah 40:3–5). He even imagines in symbolic terms that all the mountains will be flattened and all the valleys filled so that everyone will see God's glory. Many of the prophets consider that this **age to come** will happen after God has judged everyone according to their good conduct and obedience to God (Joel 2:28–32). It will be a spirit-filled time of peace and harmony when all disputes will cease (Micah 4:1–4).

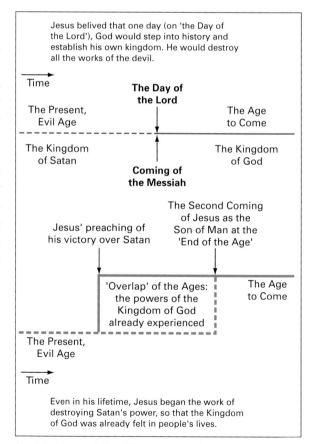

Jesus belived that one day (on 'the Day of the Lord'), God would step into history and establish his own kingdom. He would destroy all the works of the devil.

Time →

The Day of the Lord

The Present, Evil Age — The Age to Come

The Kingdom of Satan — The Kingdom of God

Coming of the Messiah

Jesus' preaching of his victory over Satan

The Second Coming of Jesus as the Son of Man at the 'End of the Age'

'Overlap' of the Ages: the powers of the Kingdom of God already experienced — The Age to Come

The Present, Evil Age

Time →

Even in his lifetime, Jesus began the work of destroying Satan's power, so that the Kingdom of God was already felt in people's lives.

Jewish ideas of the Kingdom of God as two ages.

Nation will not take up sword against nation, nor will they train for war any more.

Micah 4:3

I will pour out my Spirit on all in those days. I will show wonders in the heavens and on earth, blood and fire and billows of smoke. The sun will be turned to darkness and moon to blood before the great and dreadful day of the Lord. And everyone who calls on the name of the Lord will be saved.

Joel 2:29–32

The Old Testament prophets looked forward to a better world.

Jesus went into Galilee, proclaiming the good news of God. 'The time has come,' he said, 'the Kingdom of God is near. Repent and believe in the good news!'

Mark 1:14–15

The Kingdom of God was central to all of Jesus' teaching.

Mark makes it very clear that the good news looked forward to in the Old Testament is fulfilled in the life, death and resurrection of Jesus. It forms the heart of Jesus' teaching.

It is important to realise that the Kingdom of God is not just a reference to heaven or life after death, but is also about the relationship between God and people. Mark (1:1–20) begins his gospel by looking at the way the Kingdom of God is prepared for by John the Baptist and established by Jesus as God's Son. Becoming a member of the Kingdom of God is achieved through **baptism**.

People have long hoped that God would bring peace on earth. Do you think this could ever happen?

TASK BOX

Read Mark 1:1–20 and then answer the following questions using your own ideas:

a) Explain what the passage from the Old Testament, 'make straight paths for him', might mean.
b) Describe the role of John the Baptist.
c) What might Mark have meant when he said that the heavens were 'torn open' (1:10) at Jesus' baptism?
d) Explain why you think the fishermen followed Jesus without saying a word.
e) Is Mark telling his readers that the perfect world is here? Give reasons for your answer.

John the Baptist, the Preparer (1:2–8)

Mark quotes part of Isaiah 40:3 to show how the promise of the age to come is now beginning to happen through the teaching of John the Baptist. John is the 'messenger' or the preparer for the coming of the messiah (God's chosen one) and the long-awaited Kingdom of God.

- Mark describes John the Baptist's life as the messenger to be almost identical to that of the great Old Testament prophet Elijah who wore camel hair and a leather belt (2 Kings 1:8) and urged people of the need to repent. His food, of wild honey and locusts (1:6), is typical of the wandering holy men who lived in the wilderness. Many thought Elijah would return to announce the coming of the messiah.

- The Kingdom of God requires a radical change of belief. John the Baptist prepares for this through the symbolism of baptism or a ceremony of washing with water. Jesus' baptism marks a real change of heart where God's Spirit brings a person into a closer relationship with God. In order to receive God's Spirit a person has to prepare themselves through faith and **repentance**; it is much more than just saying sorry to someone or to God because it marks a major and real change in a person's heart, mind and everyday life.

Jesus' Baptism with the Holy Spirit (2:9–12)

From very early times it was not clear why Jesus had to be baptised by John. In Matthew's Gospel (Matthew 3:13–14), John says that Jesus should be baptising him, not the other way round. The problem is that if Jesus is sinless because he is God's Son, does he need to repent and be baptised? Perhaps Jesus' baptism marked the moment when he felt that God was calling him to begin his ministry. There are other problems with this passage. Did Jesus only become aware of his special relationship with God at his baptism? Some Christians have suggested that Jesus only became God's Son when the Spirit descended on him at his baptism. Neither of these views has been acceptable in traditional Christian teaching.

Jesus' baptism uses traditional Jewish symbols to suggest that the long-awaited moment when God's Spirit would transform the world and establish peace and harmony was beginning to happen in the life of Jesus.

- Mark says that Jesus experiences the Spirit of God as a dove, the symbol of gentleness and peace. This explains why Jesus' life and teaching on the Kingdom of God is about peace and new relationships.

The dove symbolises the presence of God's Spirit.

- The Spirit of God in the Old Testament is the creative force of God by which God created the world (Genesis 1:2), inspired his prophets (Isaiah 61:1), gave strength to men such as Samson (Judges 14:6) and would inspire the messiah to teach God's laws (Isaiah 11:2).

It is the Spirit that sends Jesus out into the wilderness to be tempted by Satan just after his baptism (1:12) and who is the means by which Jesus is able to perform his miracles. After Jesus' death, the early Christians believed that they were baptised by the Spirit to form the Church (Acts 2:1–13). This is remembered today in the festival of Pentecost. The Holy Spirit is therefore the third 'person' of the Trinity God who exists as Father, Son and Holy Spirit.

There is more discussion about Jesus' baptism in Unit 8, page 106.

Mark only gives us a very brief description of Jesus' temptations in the wilderness (1:12–13). For many who have felt powerfully called by God, there often follows a time of doubt and of wondering whether it really was God who had spoken. Jesus' forty days in the desert form a symbolic reminder that in the Old Testament the Israelites wandered in the desert before arriving at the Promised Land. They too, like Jesus, were guided by God and his angels (1:12).

The Call of the First Disciples (1:14–20)

Mark illustrates the power of the Kingdom with the dramatic change of lifestyle of Andrew, Simon, James and John. When they are called by Jesus to 'follow' (1:17) him they immediately drop their nets (1:18) and follow. It is not necessary to ask whether Jesus had taught them beforehand about the Kingdom, because the story illustrates their dramatic change of life. As 'fishers of men' (1:17) their life now is to 'fish' in a new way – they are to preach the good news of the Kingdom of God.

> **TEST YOURSELF**
>
> 1 Give two examples of the age to come as presented by some of the Old Testament prophets.
> 2 What does the dove symbolise at Jesus' baptism?
> 3 What did Jesus say he would turn the first disciples into?
> 4 Give the names of the first four disciples.

Jesus' first disciples were fishermen. Why did Jesus say to them, 'I will make you fishers of men'?

Baptism in the Church today

Baptism is the moment when a person is initiated and received into the Christian Church or community by being symbolically washed with water as a sign of purity and inner cleansing. From the very early days of Christianity, baptism was used to confirm a person's 'birth' into the promises of the new life in the Kingdom of God. St Paul writes:

We were therefore buried with him through baptism into death in order that, just as Christ was raised from the dead through glory of the Father, we too may live a new life.

Romans 6:4

Baptism today is one of the sacraments of the Church. A sacrament is often defined as 'an outward and visible sign of God's grace'. Through baptism a person 'dies' with Christ and is 'raised' with Christ. It symbolises the person's new life and commitment as a Christian. St Paul's own conversion to Christianity (Acts 9) convinced him of the reality of baptism. He felt that it was more than simply a ceremony or ritual but a *real* change only possible through belief in the resurrection of Jesus. Most Christian Churches teach that baptism is one of the two sacraments that Jesus instituted, the other being the Eucharist.

Christians have different views of when baptism takes place. For Roman Catholic, Anglican and Orthodox Churches, baptism occurs in two stages. The first is child baptism when the parents bring the child to be baptised in church by the priest. The child's parents and god-parents (or sponsors) promise to repent of their sins, turn away from evil and to bring up the child in the Christian faith until the child is

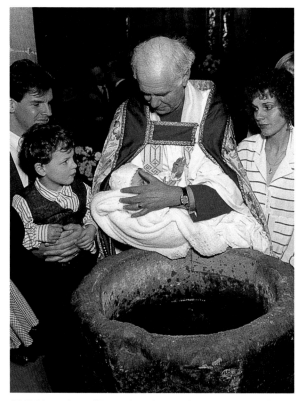

Child baptism. The priest is making the sign of the cross with water on the child's forehead.

old enough to make his or her own declaration of faith. The priest pours a few drops of water on to the forehead of the baby three times (as a sign of the Trinity) and marks it with the sign of the cross. In the Orthodox Church the whole body of the baby is dipped in water. In the Roman Catholic Church the child is also anointed with oil or chrism. Through God's grace the Spirit is present with the child until confirmation (in the Anglican, Methodist and Roman Catholic Churches) when the person is able to make their own conscious promise to turn away from evil and to accept the forgiveness of God the Father through his Son, Jesus Christ. Confirmation is carried out by a bishop who usually places his hands on the head of the person being confirmed as a blessing. For many Christians, baptism is also necessary because the gift of the Spirit is a means of removing original sin – the sin that makes all humans selfish. Without baptism no one is able to live a blameless life.

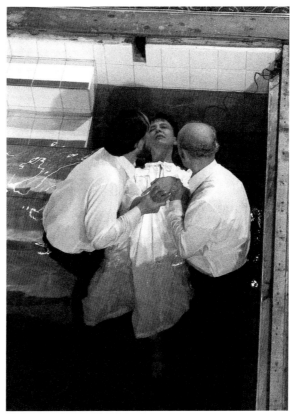

Believer's baptism.

Many Protestant Churches teach what is known as a believer's baptism. They believe that a person should make their own confession of faith when they are old enough to know what repentance means. In a typical Baptist service, for instance, the person who is being baptised makes a declaration before the congregation explaining why they want to become a Christian. The minister then totally submerges them in a pool built in the church, just as John the Baptist did in the River Jordan to those who came to be baptised by him.

Discuss whether there is any need for a ceremony of baptism if being a Christian is a matter of personal faith.

WHEN AND HOW WOULD THE KINGDOM ARRIVE?

As we have seen, Mark records that Jesus' first words were 'The Kingdom of God is near' (1:15). What exactly did Jesus mean? Undoubtedly Mark found Jesus' words just as challenging in his own day as they are to Christians today. The problem is knowing exactly what Jesus meant by the phrase 'is near'.

KEY QUESTION

What did Jesus mean when he said the 'Kingdom of God is near'?

Consider the following answers:

- Did Jesus' life and teaching begin a process (perhaps in the growth of the Church) that would eventually result in the completion of the age to come? If so, the process is not one of growth. At the moment the Church seems to be declining in the West but increasing in Africa and the East.
- Did Jesus mean that the age to come or Kingdom of God was about to arrive shortly after his death? If so, what has happened? The world is much as it has always been.
- Did Jesus mean that the Kingdom of God was really a spiritual state of mind and was 'near' for those who wished to hear it? How do we explain the gospel references to some kind of a future world disaster?

Modern scholars call the discussion of nature and the coming of the Kingdom of God **eschatology**. The problem of eschatology is not a new one and it seems that many of the writers in the New Testament struggled to understand exactly what Jesus meant when he talked of the coming of the Kingdom.

INTERPRETING THE COMING OF THE KINGDOM TODAY

There are three passages in Mark's Gospel that appear to be saying different things about the coming of the Kingdom.

> And he said to them, 'I tell you the truth, some who are standing here will not taste death before they see the Kingdom of God come with power.'
>
> *Mark 9:1*

To his disciples, Jesus seems to imply an event that will happen in their lifetime *before* they die. On the other hand, 'seeing' could be taken in a more spiritual sense of personal 'understanding' before death.

> When Jesus saw that he had answered wisely, he said to him, 'You are not far from the Kingdom of God.'
>
> And from then on no one dared ask him any more questions.
>
> *Mark 12:34*

Jesus seems to be suggesting to one of the teachers of the Law, who had grasped that love of your neighbour is the greatest commandment (12:31), that the Kingdom is a state of mind. If the lawyer lives a moral life he will 'enter' into God's love now.

On the other hand, Jesus could mean that the man's attitude is on the right lines for when the Kingdom arrives.

> Now learn this lesson from the fig-tree: As soon as its twigs get tender and its leaves come out, you know that summer is near. Even so, when you see these things happening, you know that it is near, right at the door. I tell you the truth, this generation will certainly not pass away until all these things have happened. Heaven and earth will pass away, but my words will never pass away. No one knows about that day or hour, not even the angels in heaven, nor the Son, but only the Father. Be on guard! Be alert! You do not know when that time will come.
>
> *Mark 13:28–33*

This passage comes at the end of Jesus' longest speech in the gospel (Mark 13), which is entirely concerned with the coming of the end before the age to come. Even after wars, famines, earthquakes – all of which are *signs* of the end – Mark quotes Jesus' final teaching to say that the *actual* moment of the end is unknown. What is important is to remain alert and to be morally and spiritually good.

THREE WAYS IN WHICH MODERN CHRISTIANS HAVE EXPLAINED MARK'S ESCHATOLOGY

- **Future.** The Kingdom is yet to come. Christian lifestyle should be spent in preparation, for when it arrives there will be no time to repent.
- **Inaugurated.** The Kingdom was established through Jesus' life and death. We are now living in its first phase until it is completed at the end of time when Jesus returns and God judges the world.
- **Personal.** The Kingdom is a spiritual state of mind and begins whenever a person comes to accept Jesus' teaching about God. This can be a long process of personal understanding. There is no 'event' at the end of time because this is a symbol of our own relationship with God and his judgement of us.

Three modern Christian views of the Kingdom. Why do you think they have such different interpretations?

1 What does 'Kingdom of God' mean?
2 Define 'repentance'.
3 Give two examples of the way in which baptism is practised in different ways by Christians today.
4 What is confirmation?
5 Define 'eschatology'.

REMEMBER

▶ Jesus' teaching about the Kingdom of God is *not* primarily about life after death.
▶ The Kingdom of God is God's relationship with humans through repentance and forgiveness.
▶ The problem that modern interpreters face is knowing whether the Kingdom is a personal experience of God's reality now, or a future event, or both.
▶ Baptism is the way in which someone becomes a committed Christian and 'enters' the Kingdom.

TASK BOX

a) Explain why Christians have interpreted Jesus' teaching in Mark 9:1 in different ways.
b) What is Jesus teaching about the Kingdom of God and evil through his parable of the Strongman (Mark 3:23-27)?
c) **Either**: Draw a poster or diagram entitled, 'What Christians believe about the Kingdom of God'.
Or: Write an essay: 'The Kingdom of God is just about one's personal relationship with God.' Discuss.

WEBLINKS

※ Christian teaching on the Trinity: www.gbible.org/doctrine_of_the_trinity.htm
※ Believer's baptism: http://ourworld.compuserve.com/homepages/cphicks/tbcbapt4.htm
※ Roman Catholic teaching on child baptism: www.catholic.com/library/Infant_Baptism.asp

---

1 Outline **two** features of infant baptism. [2]
2 Explain why some Christians prefer to be baptised as adults. [6]
3 What happened at Jesus' baptism according to Mark's Gospel? [7]
4 'You don't need to be specially washed in a ceremony to become a Christian.' Do you agree? Give reasons for your answer, showing that you have thought about more than one point of view. [5]

Assignment

UNIT THREE | Parables and the Kingdom of God

3

WHY DID JESUS USE PARABLES?

Jesus frequently used **parables** to illustrate his teaching. Parables, like all stories, are often able to convey difficult ideas through the use of metaphor (a symbol used as a comparison) or allegory (a story with many meanings). Most scholars agree that when we read or listen to the parables we are perhaps closest to hearing the actual words of Jesus. Often Jesus chose examples from everyday life in his parables to express his teaching about the Kingdom of God in a memorable as well as challenging way.

Jesus' own reason for telling parables is found in Mark 4:10–12. Parables are used to illustrate the Kingdom to those with faith or a willingness to learn. But a warning is aimed at the 'outsiders', those who are too wrapped up in their own cleverness or arrogance to understand the simple reality of the Kingdom. To them, parables are riddles or strange stories with no inner meaning. The passage in Mark is not easy. Perhaps Jesus was warning some people that faith has to be based on real understanding and that entry into the Kingdom cannot be based on outward show. It might be a sarcastic comment against those who think they can just repent at any time and be forgiven, but who have failed to realise that pretending to be religious cannot fool God.

He said to them, 'Do you bring in a lamp to put it under a bowl or a bed?'

Mark 4:21

What is this riddle asking you to think about?

Jesus used many different forms of parable depending on his audience. Sometimes a simple saying was sufficient to make the point, on other occasions it required a more complex story or allegory. All parables illustrate different aspects of the Kingdom. In fact, Mark records very few of Jesus' parables compared to Luke's Gospel. Mark makes the Sower and the Seed the most important one – by understanding this parable you will understand all the others.

Jesus said to them, 'Don't you understand this parable? How then will you understand any parable?'

Mark 4:13

Jesus said this to his own disciples about the parable of the Sower and the Seed.

Jesus' parables often tell stories, are very memorable and have inspired painters for centuries. What is this picture of one of Jesus' parables by Brueghel teaching?

TASK BOX

Read the following and answer the questions:

When he was alone, the Twelve and the others around him asked him about the parables. He told them,

'The secret of the Kingdom of God has been given to you. But to those on the outside everything is said in parables so that, "they may be ever seeing but never perceiving, and ever hearing but never understanding; otherwise they might turn and be forgiven!"'

Mark 4:10–12

a) From what you have studied so far what do you think are the 'secrets' of the Kingdom of God?
b) Give some examples of the kind of people who are on the 'outside'.
c) Why do outsiders hear Jesus' parables as riddles (translated here as 'parables')?
d) Explain what it means for outsiders to see and hear without perceiving and understanding.
e) Describe and give examples of how people today might pretend to be religious.

INTERPRETING ALLEGORIES

Allegories were often used by the Old Testament prophets as a means of preaching complex, often political, teachings. Ezekiel, for instance, gives an allegory of a valley of dry bones (Ezekiel 37). The dry bones symbolise Israel's lack of faith and a spiritually dead nation. Only when the people listen to God's Word and receive the Spirit do their bones live again and they become fully human. Jesus also used **allegory parables** to illustrate more complex aspects of the Kingdom, where each part of the allegory represents a particular idea. Mark's Gospel contains two main allegories, the Sower and the Seed (4:1–9 and 4:13-20) and the Tenants in the Vineyard (12:1–12).

Parable of the Sower (4:1–9; 13–20)

All the synoptic gospels contain the Sower and the Seed and its interpretation. In Mark it may have served to encourage those who were losing their faith through persecution and the attractions of power and wealth.

The situation is typical of everyday farming in Galilee. As the sower threw the seeds by hand they inevitably fell onto different kinds of soil. The parable relates how the seeds respond to the different conditions – the compacted soil of the path that the sower had trodden, thin soil on rocky ground and the good soil.

The allegory is an honest look at the way the Kingdom of God is and will be received by different types of people. Perhaps it encourages those who either feel that all Christians should have the same kind of faith, or who are worried that some have not responded fully to the Kingdom of God. Encouragement is given to those who have resisted the attractiveness of the materialistic life and persecution and teasing by non-Christians.

- The 'seed' (4:14) is the Word of God or the message of the gospel. But the explanation also says that the seed represents the different

Sowing by hand today in Nigeria. Jesus' parables often use timeless images.

types of people. This is confusing and may be the result of Mark or an earlier interpreter trying to explain the relationship between the message and how it has been receieved.

- The 'path' (4:15) is the path that the sower makes round the field, and so refers here to the well-worn track of everyday life. The kind of people represented by the path are those who are totally focused on their own goals and so the gospel is irrelevant to them.
- Those who are represented as the seed falling on 'rocky' ground (4:5) have no root (4:17). These are people who lack firm belief or staying power and may be those who have become Christians for social reasons but give up when their beliefs are really put to the test.
- The 'thorns' (4:7) represent all human material desires of wealth, power, influence. As the Kingdom of God is not about these things, eventually materialism destroys faith in the spiritual life.
- Interestingly, the 'good soil' (4:8) delivers up different quantities of crop (30, 60 and 100 times the original amount sown). Perhaps the teaching here is to suggest that not all Christians respond in exactly the same way to the gospel, but all flourish.

Tenants in the Vineyard (12:1–12)

The purpose of Tenants in the Vineyard is very different to the Sower and the Seed and is based on the political situation in Galilee. No explanation follows it, but by quoting the well-known Old Testament allegory in Isaiah 5 about the faithlessness of Israel, Jesus cleverly implies that this is no simple story. Jesus has taken the allegory from Isaiah and then reapplied it to his own current situation. It is a stern warning to Jewish leaders who arrogantly think that God's promise or covenant requires no effort. More significantly, he predicts their downfall.

The setting in everyday life refers to the fact that absentee landlords owned many vineyards in Galilee during the first century CE, therefore the temptation was for the tenants to fail to pay rent. This was a politically dangerous decision and those who did so knew that punishments would be severe. The allegory is a sketch about the way in which the leaders of Israel have frequently ignored the teachings of the prophets about loyalty to God. The parable ends by warning that the Kingdom of God will now be offered to others, not just Jewish leaders.

- The 'man' or 'landlord' (12:1) may refer to God, who first gives his promise to the Jewish leaders and then (12:9) to others.
- 'Farmers' or 'tenants' (12:2) refers to the leaders of Israel. They clearly see the parable as aimed at them because they want to arrest Jesus when he finishes this teaching (12:12).
- 'Servants' (12:2) refers to the prophets of Israel whose job was to bring God's message to Israel. Many of them suffered badly at the hands of the leaders of Israel.
- 'Son' (12:6) refers to Jesus as the final prophet of Israel whose teaching on the Kingdom, as we have seen in the parable of the Sower, warns against arrogance, false faith and materialism, all the qualities the farmers

Olive trees in Israel today.

have shown in the story so far. The son's death refers to Jesus' own crucifixion at the hands of the Jewish leaders.

- 'Kill the tenants' (12:9) refers to God's **judgement**, either when the Kingdom arrives or as a warning that the Romans will destroy the leaders of Israel. In fact, in 70 CE Jerusalem was destroyed, so Jesus' prediction was fulfilled. But the point of the allegory is that now the promise of the Kingdom of God is given to others (12:9), in other words to ordinary Jews and non-Jews.

- 'Stone' and 'corner stone' (12:10) both refer to Jesus and his teaching on the Kingdom. Without this add-on to the main allegory the story would have ended with the death of the son and with no reference to the significance of his death and the resurrection. The 'corner stone' in many buildings is the biggest and most important stone, which supports the rest of the structure. Therefore the rejected stone has become the foundation of a new religious tradition, Christianity as represented by the Church for the past 2000 years.

A modern corner stone. Why did Jesus use the metaphor of the cornerstone in his parable?

TASK BOX

a) Design a picture or poster of the Tenants in the Vineyard and its meaning.

b) Summarise the teaching in the parable in no more than 20 words. Give it a headline suitable for a modern newspaper.

c) Choose a modern political event (e.g. a war, a rebellion, treatment of schools or hospitals) and write your own parable warning against it.

TEST YOURSELF

1 Name three different kinds of parables Jesus told.

2 What was Jesus' reason for using parables as recorded by Mark?

3 In the parable of the Sower what do each of the following represent: the seed, the birds, the stony ground, the rocky ground, the good soil?

4 In the parable of the Tenants in the Vineyard what do each of the following represent: the tenants, the owner, the servants, the son, the destruction of the vineyard?

INTERPRETING SAYINGS PARABLES

KEY QUESTION

When studying the parables should they be interpreted as having a future, inaugurated or personal view of the Kingdom of God?

Mark's main collection of parables follows after the key parable of the Sower and the Seed. The collection of **sayings parables** tells us a lot about Mark's understanding of the Kingdom of God – how it appears to be hidden or secret; why its growth is a mystery and why the final moment of God's judgement is inevitable.

The Lamp and the Lamp Stand (4:21–23)

The setting in everyday life refers to a very ordinary and common household object. It would be crazy to light a lamp and then to hide it. But that, of course, is what the parable is all about. So the riddle is why would anyone put a lamp under a bed? 'Light' refers to the final glorious state of the Kingdom or possibly to personal understanding. The parable could also be a way of encouraging those who have kept their knowledge of the Kingdom to themselves to share it with others.

A modern lamp based on an ancient design. Why is light such an important religious symbol?

The Measure (4:24–25)

A modern measuring bowl.

The setting in everyday life refers to a large bowl used for measuring grain. Jesus imagines that when a person measures out a quantity of grain he will receive it all back again and a great deal more. The 'measure' symbolises God's love and generosity. The rewards of the Kingdom of God far outweigh anything that a person could possibly contribute themselves. The parable ends with a stern warning of judgement. Those who do not give generously to others will have everything 'taken away' (4:25) from them. It is not clear when this judgement will be, but a future idea of the Kingdom of God might suggest this will be at the Last Judgement when God judges the whole world.

'With the measure you use, it will be measured to you – and even more. Whoever has will be given more; whoever does not have, even what he has will be taken from him.'

Mark 4:24–5

A New Approach – St Mark's Gospel

The Seed and Harvest Time (4:26–29)

Harvest is a symbol of God's judgement.

This parable is only found in Mark's Gospel. Perhaps it is included because it illustrates a theme that Mark finds especially important, that the presence of the Kingdom of God is a mystery.

The setting in everyday life refers to the mysterious and marvellous way in which a seed grows into a fully developed plant. The emphasis of the parable is on God's continuous presence in the world regardless of whether humans believe in him or not (4:27). The symbol of 'harvest' refers to the completion of the Kingdom of God, and the symbol of harvesting of the crop refers to God's judgement of the world.

You will have to decide which kind of eschatology suits this parable best. Does the idea of growth refer to personal understanding of God, or to the growth of the Church in the world, or to gradual preparation of the world for final judgement?

The Mustard Seed (4:30–32)

Although this parable is very similar to the Seed and Harvest Time, Mark may have included it because of the reference to the birds in the branches of the tree, which is a symbol of the inclusion of **Gentiles** into the Kingdom of God.

The setting in everyday life refers to the way in which a mustard seed grows from a very small seed into a very large plant (4:31). The reference to the 'birds' (4:32) is probably from the Old Testament book of Daniel (4:10–12). In Daniel's allegory, the tree is the one found in the Garden of Eden and the birds are the Gentiles who will be accepted into the age to come.

Again, Christians today interpret this parable in various ways. Some interpret it with an inaugurated eschatology to mean that the Kingdom of God will grow from very small beginnings until completion in the age to come. Others, taking a personal eschatological position, argue that it could be describing how a person's small amount of faith develops until they come to a full understanding of God's presence.

The fully-grown mustard seed is a symbol of completion.

TEST YOURSELF

1. What do the birds symbolise in the parable of the Mustard Seed?
2. What does harvest symbolise in the parables?
3. Give one meaning of the symbol of light in the parable of the Lamp.
4. What is the warning given in the parable of the Measure?

How to study parables:
www.discipleship.net/
parables.htm

Modern parables used by
Oxfam to encourage small-scale
producers throughout the world:
www.oxfam.org.uk/what_we_do/
fairtrade/parables/

WEBLINKS

REMEMBER

- The parables were Jesus' chief means of explaining complex ideas about the Kingdom of God.
- Many parables use examples from everyday life to illustrate the Kingdom of God.
- Mark considers the parable of the Sower and the Seed to be a summary of all the main ideas found in the other parables.
- Christians today still debate whether the Kingdom of God is a personal experience, a way of talking about the development of the Church or a future event at the end of time.

---

1 a. (i) Outline the teaching about the Kingdom of God in the parables of Mark's Gospel.
   (ii) Explain the differences between a parable and an allegory using examples from Mark's Gospel.
   (iii) Explain the use of parables in Mark's Gospel. [12]

  b. 'This earth will never be God's Kingdom.'
     Do you agree? Give reasons for your opinion, showing you have considered another point of view. In your answer you should refer to Mark's Gospel. [8]

2 a. Outline the parable Jesus told where he compared the Kingdom of God to a mustard seed. [4]

  b. Explain why some Christians today believe the Kingdom of God is a personal experience. [3]

  c. Why did Jesus use parables to teach about the Kingdom of God? [3]

  d. 'Jesus' parables make it difficult to understand the Kingdom of God.'
     Do you agree? Give reasons for your answer, showing that you have thought about more than one point of view. [5]

Assignment

UNIT FOUR | Miracles and the Kingdom of God

4

KEY WORDS

Exorcism: A special form of healing when an evil spirit is expelled from a person (or place).

Fundamentalist, literalist, conservative and liberal: Different modern Christian interpretations of miracles.

Healing miracle: A moment when a person's illness is removed by Jesus as God's Son and they feel restored. In Mark these are also symbols of the Kingdom of God.

Miracle: A moment when God acts in a powerful and special way in the world.

Nature miracles: A special moment when Jesus as God's Son alters the laws of nature for human advantage.

MIRACLES AS SIGNS OF GOD'S PRESENCE IN THE WORLD

Miracles are dramatic or spectacular moments that illustrate the reality of the Kingdom and the role of Jesus as God's chosen one.

KEY QUESTION

Why does God perform miracles?

In the first century, many Jewish writers considered that when the messiah appeared God would perform special miracles as signs that the age to come was about to arrive. But in the Old Testament, miracles such as the Crossing of the Red Sea (Exodus 14) or the Giving of Bread in the Wilderness (Exodus 16) were understood to be signs of God's special commitment to the Jewish people. Miracles, therefore, were not just spectacular events, but moments of symbolic importance. The Giving of Bread in the Wilderness, for instance, not only represents God's love and care for his people, but is also a sign of the giving of the Law to Moses later on. Bread therefore symbolises God's care for the body and for the soul.

Mark is also aware that Jesus' miracles are very much like his parables; miracles express some powerful ideas about the nature of the Kingdom of God. In some ways, miracles are parables that

are acted out. In fact, as Mark places Jesus' first major miracle immediately after his collection of parables in Chapter 4, it is clear that he wants his readers to think of the miracles as a continuation of Jesus' teaching on the Kingdom of God. We will see that miracles always have some special teaching purpose.

Types of miracles Jesus performed

Healing miracles. Mark records only a few of Jesus' healing miracles but he does suggest that Jesus frequently cured people's physical illnesses (Mark 1:32–34). It appears to have been one of his special gifts. In the first century, people often believed that illness was the result of sin, so when Jesus cured illness he was also forgiving them. Healings therefore symbolise the healing of the whole person.

Exorcism miracles. Exorcisms are another kind of healing. People in the first century often believed that mental illness was the result of being possessed by a demon or evil spirit, and Mark records Jesus having to exorcise or throw out many demons.

Nature miracles. Nature miracles do not directly involve people. They are moments when the ordinary laws of physics are altered or suspended.

Interpreting the miracle of the Calming of the Storm

To understand the Calming of the Storm properly we have to remember that a person living in the first century would not only have had a less sophisticated scientific understanding of the world than we have today, but they would also have connected the story with other acts of God that the Old Testament records. In other words, the storm is a symbol both of evil *and* human failure to trust God.

The miracle is about God's love and ability to overcome fear. It is a sign, therefore, of the calm and peace that the Kingdom of God will bring.

Calming of the Storm

That day when evening came, he said to his disciples, 'Let us go over to the other side.' Leaving the crowd behind, they took him along, just as he was, in the boat. There were also other boats with him. A furious squall came up, and the waves broke over the boat, so that it was nearly swamped. Jesus was in the stern, sleeping on a cushion. The disciples woke him and said to him, 'Teacher, don't you care if we drown?'

He got up, rebuked the wind and said to the waves, 'Quiet! Be still!' Then the wind died down and it was completely calm.

He said to his disciples, 'Why are you so afraid? Do you still have no faith?'

They were terrified and asked each other, 'Who is this? Even the wind and waves obey him!'

Mark 4:35–41

First-Century Beliefs

In order to understand the miracle properly we have to understand what kind of things people believed in the first century when the story was told and written down.

- In Jewish thought, the sea or the 'deep' were the deep waters below the earth, often thought to be the dwelling place of evil spirits. When the sea became choppy, some of the more superstitious people thought the evil spirits had bubbled up to the surface and were attacking them. The sea also symbolised the problems that good people have to face in this life (Psalm 104:5–9).
- Jesus sleeping is a sign of his absolute trust in God (Psalm 3:5). In this case, Jesus' sleep illustrates his relationship with God as Father.
- The 'storm' or 'squall' represents the battle between good (from the heavens) and evil (from the deep waters below).
- The sense that God has deserted the writer is a theme of many of the Psalms. The disciples' fear is because they feel that God is 'asleep' and has forgotten them in their trouble (Psalm 44:23).
- 'Be still' could also be translated as 'be silent' because Jesus is speaking to the evil spirits of the storm. The story is also a kind of exorcism.
- 'Do you still have no faith?' is a theme of many of the Psalms – the writers feel that even a belief in God is not always enough when it is tested by hostile people or moments of extreme suffering and terror.
- The great calm after the storm symbolises the triumph of good over evil and the complete peace that only God can bring. This is the peace that will be experienced in the age to come in the Kingdom of God (discussed in Unit 2). The Psalms sometimes use this metaphor to express a restored faith in God.

Later Christians took some of the ideas even further and suggested that the boat is a symbol of the Church and the difficult times that the Church often goes through in the world.

a) What does the story of the Calming of the Storm teach about the Kingdom of God?

b) What does the story of the Calming of the Storm teach about Jesus?

c) Read Mark 6:45–51 when Jesus walks on the water. It is a very similar story.

Explain the symbolism of Jesus walking on the water from what you have learnt about interpreting the Calming of the Storm.

Consider how the artist has emphasised the faith of the disciples with Jesus during the storm.

Jesus walking on water.

KEY QUESTION

Has modern science made belief in miracles impossible for Christians today?

Is it possible for God to suspend the laws of nature for some special reason? For many Christians the answer is 'yes', because if God were not able to do this then he would not be God. The purpose of Jesus' miracles was to show that as it was God who was performing the miracles, so Jesus was God's Son. It is true that in the Old Testament the prophets performed miracles, and later Jesus' own disciples were also able to perform miracles, but in these cases it was not they who performed, but God acting on their requests. However, the problem for many today is that we can give different explanations for these moments, based on superior knowledge of the way the world works. The following show how we explain these moments:

- Healing miracles can often be explained because the human mind can have great power over the body.
- Evil spirits are old-fashioned ways of explaining depression, mental illness, anxieties and so on. Exorcisms were just means of helping the person overcome their fears and giving them peace of mind.
- Nature miracles can often be explained by looking for causes in nature that might have been overlooked. There is also a tendency for people to exaggerate events and to elaborate details that were not there at the original moment.

In Unit 1 we looked at three different ways in which Christians have interpreted the gospels. Now let us see how each approaches the problem of miracles. We must not forget that each view shares many of the ideas of the others. In practice it would be unusual to find someone who exactly fitted into one of these categories.

Fundamentalist Christian View of Miracles

The **fundamentalist** and **literalist** takes the text pretty much word for word as the actual sayings and actions of Jesus. They understand a miracle to be the action of God in history and in nature, bringing about a special, unexpected or impossible outcome. Nature miracles are of particular significance for the fundamentalist Christian because they illustrate God's special power working uniquely through Jesus (Mark 6:14) to demonstrate that he is God's Son. Miracles, therefore, are a means of increasing faith, because those who had faith in Jesus were able to experience the power of God working in them.

Conservative Christian View of Miracles

The **conservative** theologian agrees that God can suspend the laws of nature, but also feels that some elements have become exaggerated over time. The miracle stories are also used to teach, and act as the means for encouraging faith. This means that although we can be sure that the miracles occurred we can't always be entirely certain what happened. The real miracle is often to be seen in the amazement of those who were affected by Jesus' personality and saw that God was somehow working through him. This is why Mark often says that the reaction of the people to Jesus' miracles was wonder and awe. This can be seen in questions such as, 'Where does he get his authority from?' and 'What is this new teaching?' (Mark 1:27).

Liberal Christian View of Miracles

The **liberal** theologian finds it totally unacceptable to believe in a God who can interfere or suspend the laws of nature. The real 'miracle' lies in a person's own realisation of something profoundly new about God. The liberal therefore stresses the symbolism of a miracle. Miracles are really types of parables. For example, when Jesus cures a blind person, his new sight is a symbol of his new understanding; a lame person who is able to walk is a symbol of a person who can now cope with the realities of life. The liberal Christian points out that there is no one word for miracle in the gospels; words used are 'amazing moments', 'powerful moments' and 'signs'. Translators often give them all one word, 'miracle', which is therefore misleading.

Modern views about the Gospel miracles

'I use the word *Miracle* to mean an interference with Nature by supernatural power. Unless there exists, in addition to Nature, something else which we may call the supernatural, there can be no miracles.'

C S Lewis, *Miracles*

'In both the Old and New Testaments miracles were *revelations*, that is to say, something was visible or experiencible in them which was hidden before; the people involved recognised and understood something which was of the greatest importance for their whole lives ... Miracles were interpreted as signs, just because they contained something which had to be understood. They were signs of the presence of God in the world at that particular moment.'

E and M-L Keller, *Miracles in Dispute*

'Today our screens are full of computer-generated graphics. An artist uses computer graphics to generate images, frame by frame. Usually, of course, the pictures are stored and played back time after time. But imagine an artist doing that live! If the artist stopped, then the image too would disappear. In a similar way, God can be thought of as sustaining the world second by second. This view of God constantly active in the creation results in a very different view of miracles from that of 'intervention'. Miracles are not God intervening where he does not usually act, but God acting in different ways from the usual ... Perhaps the *normal* and the *unusual*, or the *ordinary* and *extraordinary* acts of God would more closely mirror the Bible's teaching than "natural" and "supernatural" .'

Michael Poole, *A Guide to Science and Belief*

'Whatever else may be said, then, about the miracle stories of the gospels, it cannot be maintained that in themselves they prove the *uniqueness* of Jesus.'

Hugh Anderson, *The Gospel of Mark*

How would you define a miracle?
Which of the views above do you most agree with? Give reasons for your choice.

NATURE MIRACLES

Mark twice tells us a story about feeding a large crowd (just as he told the storm story twice). In the first case, Jesus feeds over 5000 people (Mark 6:30–43), and in the second, over 4000 (Mark 8:1–11). It is not always entirely clear why the story is repeated but it may be that Mark wanted to stress that Jesus' feedings were a standard and important feature of his teaching. Feeding as a banquet was a symbol of the Jewish age to come when there would be plenty to feed everybody. This would have been especially significant to the poor people of Galilee where the story is set. They might, therefore, have been aware that in some Jewish traditions there was an idea that Moses would return and bring with him special bread, just as he had done in the exodus. This would be the start of the Kingdom and a sign of the abundance of God's love and grace.

Interpreting the Feeding of the 5000 Today

How have Christians explained Jesus' feeding?

- A **fundamentalist** would want to highlight what it tells the reader about Jesus' divinity and his ability to feed so many with so little (two fish and five loaves). Jesus is presented as a shepherd (the people are like sheep without a shepherd), which in the Old Testament was a symbol of the messiah or even God. For example, Psalm 23 says, 'The Lord is my shepherd…'. Therefore Christians are called to preach faith in Jesus as God's Son as the only way in which God will continue to act in the world and establish his Kingdom.

- A **conservative** might wish to add that the miracle also centres around people being willing to share the little they had with one another. The miracle is that the Kingdom of God comes about when people care unselfishly for one another, just as Jesus did. Jesus 'blesses-breaks-distributes' the bread just as he does at the Last Supper (Mark 14:22–25), because both meals are symbolic of the way Christians should behave all the time. The miracle should inspire Christians today to feed the poor, or to redistribute wealth or simply to be more generous with their resources.

- A **liberal** might go further and suggest that there is more symbolism – making the story much more political for Christians today. In the Old Testament, Moses fed the people in the wilderness with the bread (or manna) God sent (Exodus 16) and then he was given a new Law comprising the Ten Commandments. Jesus is therefore a new Moses, and the bread which he gives is a symbol of the new law of love that he teaches. The reference to the five loaves is not an accident because it is symbolic of the five books of Law which Moses received. Now the five law books are replaced with one law – love. This is shown in the way people are sitting down together and sharing everything. This is how society should be at this moment. One further symbol is that 12 baskets of food are left over. In the Old Testament there were 12 tribes of Israel, but now this symbolises Jesus' 12 apostles who are the founders of the Church. Christians today are called to create a new society based on new laws of equality and tolerance.

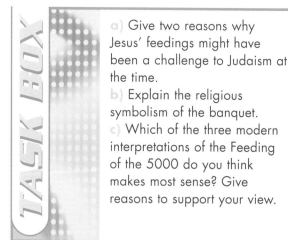

TASK BOX

a) Give two reasons why Jesus' feedings might have been a challenge to Judaism at the time.

b) Explain the religious symbolism of the banquet.

c) Which of the three modern interpretations of the Feeding of the 5000 do you think makes most sense? Give reasons to support your view.

TEST YOURSELF

1 Give an example of a nature miracle.
2 What do the disciples say to Jesus during the storm on the lake?
3 What did Jesus say to the storm when he was in the boat?
4 How does Jesus criticise the disciples after the storm is over?
5 What are the people compared to just before the feeding of the 5000?
6 How many loaves and fishes did Jesus use to feed the 5000 people?
7 Who gives the people bread to eat in the wilderness in the Old Testament?
8 How many baskets were filled after the feeding of 5000?

HEALING MIRACLES

KEY QUESTION

What kind of faith do healing miracles require?

Jesus' healing miracles served a number of purposes. Firstly, they were a means of showing how the Kingdom of God would be a time of physical and spiritual perfection. The themes of many of his healings are transformation from the old to the new. Perhaps the most spectacular miracle is the cure of Jairus' daughter who is presumed dead. Jesus 'resurrects' her as a sign of what will happen after death to those who have faith, and as a pointer towards his own resurrection. But as liberal Christians comment, the real transformation is the triumph of hope and faith over despair.

Secondly, the healing miracles mostly deal with the nature of faith. Healings are always to be seen at two levels: the healing of the body and the healing of the spirit. In other words, the miracles indicate that the whole person is always involved. Notice that in almost every case it is a person's faith that precedes the cure. This is, after all, what the Kingdom of God is about: a person's relationship with God. In the first century, the connection between illness and state of mind was far closer than we allow today. A cure is only possible through a person's repentance (change of mind) and faith.

Jesus' desire was always to treat people at their own level of belief. But faith need not be total or absolute. The teaching element in Jesus' healings clearly indicates that there are various levels of belief: from faith which is barely noticeable (Woman with Bleeding – see pages 40–41) to utter trust (Blind Bartimaeus – see page 42). Jesus indicated in the parable of the Sower that not all people will have 100 per cent faith, in order to participate in the Kingdom of God.

The healings therefore are an important indication of Jesus' own attitude to all types within society, especially those who were considered social misfits and outsiders. The healing miracles continue to have a social message for Christians today: that the Kingdom is not exclusive or limited to a few good people. Miracles continue to teach how a Christian should treat others.

> Be strong, do not fear; your God will come, he will come with vengeance; with divine retribution he will come to save you. Then will the eyes of the blind be opened and the ears of the deaf unstopped. Then will the lame leap like a deer, and the mute tongue shout for joy.

Isaiah 35:5–6

Isaiah's vision of the age to come was a time of physical and spiritual wholeness. See how Mark shows how this vision was fulfilled in Jesus' healings.

Here are three examples of healings from Mark's Gospel: Jairus' Daughter and the Woman with Bleeding; the Syro-Phoenician Woman; Blind Bartimaeus.

Jairus' Daughter and the Woman with Bleeding (5:21–43)

Here are two stories that Mark has probably joined together to illustrate different types of faith from different members of Jewish society. The story of the woman with internal bleeding also acts as a means of delaying Jesus' journey to Jairus' house, so that by the time he gets there, the child is dead.

The Woman with Bleeding suffers from two problems. Firstly, there is the affliction of her illness. It seems that she has suffered for 12 years (5:25) from internal bleeding. Although Mark doesn't describe her state of mind we can imagine how she must have felt. Furthermore she has spent all her money on useless cures (5:26). She is mentally, physically and financially at rock bottom. Secondly, according to Jewish law (Leviticus 15:25–27), a woman who is having her period is considered during that time to be unclean and cannot be touched, so she is a religious outcast.

There are two points of teaching here:

- What kind of faith does the woman have? She certainly has faith, but it is one that is born out of a certain amount of desperation. Does she think Jesus' cloak has magical powers, because she says, 'If I just touch his clothes, I will be healed' (5:28)? It is hard to know. What is important is that Jesus' treatment of her is one of generosity. Whatever her motives, he forgives her and she is healed spiritually and physically. For modern Christians, the story teaches them not to be judgemental. It is very easy to say that a person's faith is not pure or good enough or that their motives for being members of a church are not entirely clear. The story illustrates a need to be generous and tolerant.
- For many modern Christian feminists, the most important aspect of the story is that it shows Jesus overcoming centuries of sexism and prejudice against women. Jesus ignores

the laws of Leviticus, and by calling her 'daughter' (5:34) accepts her for what she is. He ignores the fact that having touched the woman he would now become technically unclean. There are still many ways in which men mistreat and discriminate against women's bodies today, and they are not always obvious (for example pornography, types of jobs and expectations in relationships).

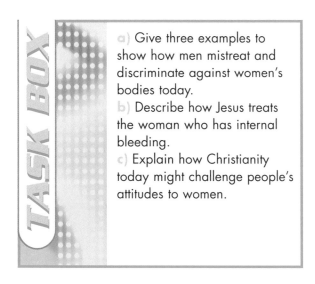

TASK BOX

a) Give three examples to show how men mistreat and discriminate against women's bodies today.
b) Describe how Jesus treats the woman who has internal bleeding.
c) Explain how Christianity today might challenge people's attitudes to women.

By contrast, the story of Jairus is about a man who is priviledged, rather than low down in society. He is one of the local synagogue leaders and responsible for its running. He must have been very well regarded by the locals, for as soon as they hear of his daughter's death they indicate their grief and despair with a great deal of crying and wailing (5:39). The story is about testing one's beliefs at such moments of despair, especially in the central Christian belief of resurrection.

- Jesus tells Jairus, 'Don't be afraid; just believe' (5:36). Jairus' initial belief is now severely challenged. Not only is his daughter dead but he has to believe, when Jesus says his daughter is not really dead but 'sleeping', that this is not a ridiculous idea as the local people clearly think (5:40). After all, he has his reputation to maintain.
- What does Jesus mean when he says the child is asleep (5:39)? Some people think he was trying to give the parents hope by saying that

the child wasn't really dead but in some kind of coma. Alternatively, Jesus was supporting a current Jewish view (held by the Pharisees) that at death the soul 'sleeps' until it is resurrected into the age to come. Jesus is encouraging Jairus to remain firm to his convictions, even if thinks he will lose his reputation.

■ The story presents modern Christians with considerable problems. For the fundamentalist or traditionalist it confirms Jesus as God's Son, for only God can give life (Job 1:21). But for liberals, even modern examples of those who have recovered from apparent death are not sufficient to convince them that this was really a miracle. What happened is less important than the symbol of the power of faith to transform despair into hope.

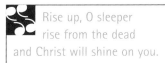

Rise up, O sleeper
rise from the dead
and Christ will shine on you.

Ephesians 5:14

In this early Christian hymn the dead are described as those who are asleep until they are resurrected to be with Christ.

'This child is not dead but asleep.' What did Jesus mean?

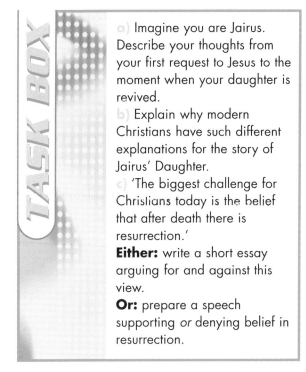
Syro-Phoenician Woman (7:24–30)

Although this story is really an exorcism (the child is possessed by an evil spirit), Mark is not interested in the details of the cure so much as the conversation between Jesus and the woman. Living in the north just beyond Palestine, the woman had probably heard about Jesus from travellers who had journeyed up from Galilee. The story has two aims.

Firstly, it is an example of the woman's strong faith because, as a Gentile, she believes that Jesus can cure her daughter at a distance.

Secondly, it marks a change in Jesus' attitude to the place of Gentiles in the Kingdom of God. This is a difficult part of the story and really depends on how you interpret the conversation between Jesus and the woman. Is she pointing out to Jesus that his attitude to the Gentiles is prejudiced and typical of Jewish attitudes to non-Jews? Or is Jesus testing her faith and seeing whether she can cope with his teasing?

The key elements of the conversation are:

- When Jesus says 'First let the children eat all they want' (7:27) he repeats a standard Jewish view that the Jews, as the children of God, will be the first to enter the Kingdom.
- The pun on the word 'bread' (7:27) refers to the teaching of Jesus. In Judaism it could refer to the Law, so here Jesus' teaching represents the New Law.
- Jesus uses the rather unpleasant term 'dog' when he says that the bread should not be tossed 'to their dogs' (7:27). It was used by Jews to describe Gentiles. He appears to say that Gentiles are not good enough to receive the teaching on the Kingdom.
- The woman returns Jesus' proverb with a clever reply, 'Even the dogs under the table eat the children's crumbs' (7:28). She shows that she understands that believing in the Kingdom requires more than just a cure of her daughter. The 'crumbs' are the little bits of Jesus' teaching she has heard, and she has based her faith on this small amount of knowledge.

Blind Bartimaeus (10:46–52)

This is the final miracle that Mark records in his gospel. Perhaps he places it here because it illustrates how the true disciple should respond to Jesus. Although Bartimaeus is blind physically, and so unable to see Jesus face to face, he knows who he is through his inner sight. The miracle is a parable of faith as a complete act of trust. This is in contrast to Jesus' own disciples. Peter failed to have complete faith and denied knowing Jesus (14:66–71), and James and John failed to understand what kind of messiah Jesus was and believed that he would give them political power in the Kingdom of God (10:35–41).

- Bartimaeus uses the title 'Son of David' (10:47) because he recognises Jesus as the fulfilment of the ancient Jewish hope that the messiah would be a descendent of King David (2 Samuel 7:12–16), although he clearly does not think of him in military terms, but as one who would administer mercy and justice.
- After his cure, Bartimaeus follows Jesus 'along the road' (10:52). The early Christians were sometimes called members of the 'Way' (e.g. Acts 9:2) and so Bartimaeus' complete trust and faith are to illustrate what it means to be a disciple and member of the Way.
- Although some people have argued that Bartimaeus may have been told about Jesus and had been impressed by the reports he had heard, it is much more likely that what Mark likes about this story is that the Kingdom can be 'seen' by those with faith. As we have seen, those who are outsiders, as he calls them, are those who, although they can see in the physical sense, 'may be ever seeing but never perceiving' (4:12).

TASK BOX

a) Look back at each of the healing stories (Jairus, the Woman with Bleeding, the Syro-Phoenician Woman and Blind Bartimaeus). Using one sentence for each, describe the kind of faith each person had in Jesus.

b) Discuss which of the healing miracles are most likely to have happened as Mark records them.

Exorcisms and evil

In the first century, many people had a very real sense that the world was the battleground between good and evil. Many Jews expected that as the age to come grew closer there would be an increased activity of evil. Mark's Gospel has a profound sense that through the person of Jesus, God would overcome evil and establish the Kingdom of God. The **exorcisms** must have been frightening events and it was not always clear whose power was more awful – God's or Satan's. It might be for that reason that a rumour developed that accused Jesus of working for Satan, or Beelzebub as he was called.

> ### Key Question
> In what ways do we believe evil exists today?

Exorcism at Capernaum (1:21–28)

The first miracle that Mark records is Jesus' exorcism of a man in the synagogue at Capernaum, the town where Jesus was living. The power of his teaching causes the demons in the possessed man to shout out. They recognise Jesus as the 'Holy One of God' (1:24), or God's representative who will destroy them. Mark often reports that it is the demons who recognise Jesus' true identity whilst his disciples frequently fail to do so. Even the people in the synagogue (1:27–28) comment on the power of his teaching rather than his identity, although they seem to sense that this is not an ordinary person.

Although it is usual today to consider demon possession as a mental disorder (such as schizophrenia and epilepsy), this doesn't mean that the question of evil is any less significant. We can still say that people become obsessed or possessed by greed, power, hatred and anger. These all require powerful teaching to combat their effects.

The exorcism of the madman at the tombs in Mark is discussed in Unit 8, pages 114–15.

How do we understand demon possession today?

New Teaching (1:27–28)

Satan appears at various stages in the gospel, from the time when Jesus is tempted in the wilderness (1:12–13) to his discussion with Peter about his role as a suffering messiah (8:33). In each case what really matters is that Jesus' new teaching is seen to be the source of truth.

> The people were all so amazed, that they asked each other, 'What is this? A new teaching – and with authority! He gives orders to the evil spirits and they obey him.'
>
> *Mark 1:27–28*
>
> Jesus' teaching challenges evil.

Beelzebub Debate (3:20–30)

Mark typically places the debate about Beelzebub within a story about Jesus' state of mind. He often does this when he wants to contrast two ideas. The idea being discussed here is the source of Jesus' power to cure people. There is a very modern ring to this concern; how would we react if a member of our family or a friend seemed to have extraordinary powers of healing mental illness? Would we feel threatened by them? That is clearly what his family (including his mother and brothers) are experiencing. They think, 'He is out of his mind' (3:21). Perhaps it is they who have summoned the expert teachers of the law from Jerusalem to travel all the way to Galilee to judge whether Jesus' powers come from Satan/Beelzebub.

Jesus tells two parables or riddles to show how wrong they are:

- **The divided kingdom**. Jesus says that if he were Satan, it would be extremely unlikely that he would be destroying his own kingdom by banishing evil spirits from it.
- **The divided family**. Jesus probably tells the second riddle because it plays on the word Beelzebul (the other name for Beelzebub), which means 'Lord of the house'. If a house or family is fighting against itself it will destroy itself.

But in fact the twist is that the observation of the lawyers is right. Jesus is destroying the kingdom of Satan, not from within but from outside. His third parable is a brief allegory, the Strongman (3:27).

- The 'Strongman' is Satan and his 'house' is his kingdom.
- To 'tie up' the Strongman means to exorcise or banish evil, just as Jesus 'silences' the storm (4:39) and establishes calm. This need not just refer to Jesus' exorcism of evil spirits but to all his teaching and actions that are establishing God's Kingdom on earth.

Finally, Jesus concludes by turning the tables on the lawyers. It is they, not he, who are out of their minds as it seems that they cannot distinguish good from evil if they think he is actually working for Satan. This is true blasphemy (3:28) and not the kind of blasphemy they accuse him of doing when he cures the paralysed man (2:7). Therefore, in very strong language, Jesus concludes that so long as they have inverted good with evil they 'will never be forgiven' (3:29).

TASK BOX

a) Describe the exorcism of the epileptic boy (or the boy possessed by an evil spirit) (9:14-27).

b) Explain how you think evil is different from just being bad.

c) Take one of the following commandments (Exodus 20) and describe what life would be like today if the commandment was inverted and treated as a good thing:

- 'do not bear false witness' – 'lie'
- 'keep the Sabbath day holy' – 'do not stop working'
- 'do not kill' – 'have no respect for life'

d) Prepare for a class debate on what kind of actions or deeds can never be forgiven.

TEST YOURSELF

1 What did Jesus say to Jairus after he had been told that his daughter was dead?
2 How long has the Woman with Bleeding been ill?
3 How did Jesus treat the Woman with Bleeding who had touched him?
4 What was the Syro-Phoenician Woman's reply to Jesus' testing question?
5 What title does Blind Bartimaeus use to address Jesus?
6 What do evil spirits recognise about Jesus?
7 Why do the teachers of the law think Jesus is Beelzebub?
8 Outline Jesus' parable of the Strongman.

---

1 a. Describe Mark's account of the healing of a paralysed man. [5]

  b. Explain how the story might teach Christians about the importance of faith in their lives today. [7]

  c. 'Christians must believe that Jesus' healing miracles must have happened.'
  Do you agree? Give reasons to support your answer and show that you have thought about different points of view. [5]

2 a. Jesus' disciples tried to heal an epileptic boy. Outline the conversation that followed between Jesus and the boy's father. [4]

  b. Explain how Christians today understand demon possession. [3]

  c. Jesus fed 5000 people. What does this miracle teach about the Kingdom of God? [3]

  d. 'The Kingdom of God is yet to arrive.'
  Do you agree? Give reasons for your answer, showing that you have thought about more than one point of view. [5]

Assignment

🕷 Fundamentalist Christian claims about healing miracles today:
www.christian-faith.com/html/page/people_healed

🕷 Jesus as Son of God:
www.bbc.co.uk/religion/programmes/sog/

WEBLINKS

REMEMBER

▸ Miracles are considered by Mark to be powerful moments of God's action in the world.

▸ Healing miracles are possible because of a person's faith.

▸ Miracles are a sign of Jesus' authority as God's Son and messiah.

▸ Miracles are like parables and are designed to teach about the Kingdom of God.

5

KEY WORDS

Apostles: Jesus chose some of his closest disciples (the 12) to continue his teaching and be an example after his death (Judas was replaced by Matthias). An apostle means literally 'one who is sent' and has also come to refer to anyone who has brought Christianity to a country.

Church: This can be used in two senses. The Church refers to all Christians throughout the world. A church is a building where people worship. Church is used mostly in its first meaning throughout this book.

Disciple: Anyone who follows the example and teaching of Jesus.

Praxis: This term means 'faith in action'. Feeding the poor and upholding justice in society are two examples of Christian praxis.

Vocation: Means that someone feels that they are being called by God to carry out a particular task or job.

THE NEW COMMUNITY

As we have seen in Unit 2, the Kingdom of God is closely associated with the creation of a new society. Almost everything that Mark records of Jesus' teaching describes how this new community will work. What attitudes will people need to become members of it, and what attitudes are unacceptable? Although the term is never used in the gospel, this new community is what we would now call the **Church** – the worldwide community of Christians.

> ### KEY QUESTION
> What are the personal qualities of the true disciple?

The very early Christians called themselves people of 'the Way'. At Caesarea Philippi (8:27–33) Jesus taught that the life of a **disciple** must be like his own, which is a journey to the cross. As he says, a disciple must 'take up his cross and follow' (8:34). This could be taken just as a metaphor meaning that Christianity is about sacrifice for others, commitment and love, but during Mark's time under the persecution by the Roman emperor Nero (64 CE), it would certainly

have been understood much more literally as referring to the ultimate sacrifice of martyrdom. There are many other moments in Jesus' teaching when it is difficult to tell whether he means what he says literally or metaphorically.

A disciple is a person who follows Jesus and is a member of the new community. Mark's Gospel is often very critical of Jesus' own disciples, as we shall see. So, it is often debatable whether Mark considered Jesus' life an ideal which no one could really achieve, or whether in fact Jesus actually did expect his followers to match his example. The theme of discipleship is important throughout Mark's Gospel.

THE NATURE OF DISCIPLESHIP

Jesus used all kinds of images to convey the serious demands that the Kingdom of God would make of those who chose this way of life. Some make for awkward reading, like this passage from Mark 9:42–48 which talks about the action a false disciple should take if he causes someone else to sin.

The nature of true discipleship is vocation and repentance, being called to preach, leadership, example and humility.

And if anyone causes one of these little ones who believe in me to sin, it would be better for him to be thrown into the sea with a large millstone tied around his neck. If your hand causes you to sin, cut it off. It is better for you to enter life maimed than with two hands to go into hell, where the fire never goes out. And if your foot causes you to sin, cut it off. It is better for you to enter life crippled than to have two feet and be thrown into hell. And if your eye causes you to sin, pluck it out.

Mark 9:42–47

a) Who do you think the 'little ones' are?
b) What do the metaphors or symbols of cutting off hands and feet and plucking out eyes mean?
c) Discuss whether you think this passage should be read literally.

Vocation and Repentance

> ### KEY QUESTION
>
> What is the difference between a job and a vocation?

The primary quality of the disciple or follower is repentance. As John the Baptist and then Jesus taught, without repentance or a complete change of mind and heart (1:15) a person is not seeing the world from the perspective of the Kingdom of God. But repentance alone is not enough. An inner change must also bring with it what modern Christians call **praxis** or practical change. This is the desire to want to change not only one's own lifestyle but also the nature of society as a whole.

But repentance cannot happen unless a person feels called to change their lifestyle. This is what **vocation** means.

The opening of Mark's Gospel gives a few selected examples. After the call of his own group of the first disciples (1:14–20), Mark tells the story of the Call of Levi (2:13–17). Levi is both a Jew and a tax-collector, and as an

Jesus' eats with the tax collector Levi. Having a meal is a sign of fellowship. Why was this provocative?

employee of the Romans he would have been regarded as a traitor by most Jews. Furthermore, tax-collectors had a reputation for over taxing and pocketing the surplus. The Jewish teachers called these people 'sinners', because they did not keep to the Torah. Therefore they would never be able to have the rewards of the age to come when it arrived nor the promises of paradise. Yet these are the very people (such as prostitutes and lepers) to whom Jesus first addressed the gospel.

> 'Why does he eat with tax collectors and "sinners"?' On hearing this, Jesus said to them, 'It is not the healthy who need a doctor, but the sick. I have not come to call the righteous, but sinners.'
>
> *Mark 2:16–17*
>
> Jesus' reply to the teachers of the law. Who do you think Jesus thought the sick were?

A vocation means literally to be called by God. Before a person can offer themselves to be a priest or a Church minister, they have to convince others in the Church that they have a genuine calling or vocation. But vocations need not only be directed specifically to the Church. Teachers, lawyers, social workers and members of parliament, for example, might all feel that their particular calling is to serve the community in some special way as Christians.

Preaching and Mission

KEY QUESTION

Should Christians convert non-Christians to Christianity?

Jesus taught that the gospel is not an academic idea, like learning History or Physics, the Kingdom of God is to be preached. The Christian's duty is also to announce the good news. This can be done in the obvious sense of preaching or evangelism, but it is clear from Mark's Gospel that it can also be achieved through living as an example to others.

Jesus' 12 disciples (6:6–13) were sent out to preach with a stick, tunic and sandals but no food or money. As some of them were fishermen they were certainly not poor, so Jesus' demands on them were really a challenge to their commitment and to a new way of life. As Jesus had said to his first disciples, they were to adapt their skills as fishermen and become, instead 'fishers of men' (1:17) – preaching to people and gathering them together to form the new community.

> As Jesus walked beside the Sea of Galilee, he saw Simon and his brother Andrew casting a net into the lake, for they were fishermen. 'Come, follow me', Jesus said, 'and I will make you fishers of men.' At once they left their nets and followed him.
>
> *Mark 1:17–18*

Jesus' final instruction to them was that they were to 'shake the dust from under their feet' (6:11) at the villages that did not listen to them. Every Jew returning to Palestine shook the dust from Gentile lands off his feet before re-entering the country. The sign indicates that the village is no longer to be considered part of the Christian community. This is not an easy passage to understand but it does indicate that being part of the Christian community requires dedication and commitment. The role of the disciples as missionaries (6:12–13) was to imitate Jesus and:

- preach and call people to repent
- drive out evil spirits
- cure the sick.

Mission and work of the Church today

After the resurrection, the risen Jesus said to the disciples, 'Go into all the world and preach the good news to all creation' (Mark 16:15). The Church has always seen itself therefore as the organisation that has carried out Jesus' command.

Those who preach might feel that they do so because, like the disciples, they have a special calling or vocation to do so. They might be ordained priests or ministers, lay preachers or Readers (in the Anglican Church), nuns and monks. But preaching repentance is not just a role for a few. In Mark 13:10, Jesus suggests that all Christians are preaching the gospel whenever they stand up for their Christian beliefs and set an example, especially in a society that is hostile to religious beliefs.

In the nineteenth century, missionaries took the idea of mission much more literally and went out to non-Christian countries to convert them – they frequently built schools and hospitals in order to do this. Today, missionary societies such as the Anglican missionary organisation USPG (United Society for the Propagation of the Gospel) and the Council for World Mission are much more conscious of allowing people to maintain their local customs and are less aggressive in their missionary work, but they continue to provide education, healthcare and aid in times of disasters. One of the most famous missions was founded in 1952 when Mother Teresa of Calcutta set up her Missionaries of Charity for her nuns to help the sick and dying in Calcutta.

But it is not just missionaries who carry out the command to heal. For centuries the Church has been the main provider of care for the sick. Many hospitals are named after saints and organisations, such as Trinity Hospice (founded in 1891 and the oldest in England), and provide care for the terminally ill and dying. Emmaus, which was founded in 1942, helps the homeless through its Emmaus communities.

The mission of the Church is carried out through preaching the gospel against injustice, exploitation of the weak, prejudice against race and sex, and by providing aid for the poor. There are many Church organisations and communities dedicated to this work, such as Corrymeela in Northern Ireland, which since the Second World War has worked to enable Protestant and Roman Catholics to understand each other better and to break down prejudices of young and old at school and in the local community.

CORRYMEELA IS PEOPLE OF ALL AGES AND CHRISTIAN TRADITIONS, WHO, INDIVIDUALLY AND TOGETHER ARE COMMITTED TO THE HEALING OF SOCIAL, RELIGIOUS & POLITICAL DIVISIONS THAT EXIST IN NORTHERN IRELAND AND THROUGHOUT THE WORLD

TEST YOURSELF

1 Define 'disciple'.
2 What does 'praxis' mean?
3 Give an example of a vocation.
4 What did Jesus say should happen to those who caused the 'little ones' to sin?
5 Why was Jesus criticised for eating with Levi?
6 What was Jesus' reply to those who criticised him for eating with Levi?
7 Name two things the 12 disciples were to do when they went out to preach.
8 Define 'apostle'.
9 What did Jesus say the apostles were to do if a place rejected their preaching?

Leadership and Example

Jesus chose 12 disciples (3:13–19), like the 12 tribes of ancient Israel, to symbolise the new Israel – the new community of people without the need for land and power. Peter and the inner group of Andrew, James and John represent those who were closest to him. All were given authority to exorcise evil spirits as a symbol of the power of the Kingdom and as a sign that repentance brings with it a complete renewal of body and mind. This is why Mark calls them **apostles**, because they are 'sent out' (which is what the word means) as founders of the Church.

■ Simon is given the name Peter which means 'the rock'. In Matthew's Gospel, Jesus says that Peter's new name is a symbol of his role as leader or 'rock' of the church after Jesus' death. Some suggest that his new name also refers to his reliable character as a man of faith – even though later Peter denies knowing Jesus three times.

■ James and John's surname, Thunder, may refer to their style of preaching. But they were not without their faults, because later they completely misunderstand the nature of the community and want Jesus to give them important places within it (10:35–40).

■ Simon the Zealot's name may indicate that he was zealous or ambitious for a new kind of Kingdom. Like James and John he may well have expected a political-type kingdom.

■ Judas is singled out by Mark as the one who ultimately betrayed Jesus. It is possible that his surname, Iscariot, could mean 'sword-bearer' – the title given to some of the Zealots who fought for religious and political freedom.

Humility

In Mark 10:13–16, Jesus' teaching is aimed at members of the community whose behaviour has become arrogant and insensitive. The disciples lack humility.

> People were bringing little children to Jesus to have him touch them, but the disciples rebuked them. When Jesus saw this, he was indignant. He said to them, 'Let the little children come to me, and do not hinder them, for the Kingdom of God belongs to such as these. I tell you the truth, anyone who will not receive the Kingdom of God like a little child will never enter it.' And he took the children in his arms, put his hands on them and blessed them.
>
> *Mark 10:13–16*

■ Mark probably included the story to reprimand those in his community who were over-stepping their authority and whose prejudices had got the better of them. Children were brought to be blessed by their elders on the Jewish Day of Atonement, but the disciples clearly think Jesus is far too important to be bothered by this custom.

Why did the disciples criticise people for bringing children to Jesus? Why did Jesus choose a child to be a symbol of discipleship?

- Mark reminds us that Jesus' concern for those who traditionally in Jewish society had few legal and religious rights, such as children, are in fact examples of what all true disciples should be like.

- Entering the Kingdom and being part of the Christian community is not based on rational and strict rule-based adult expectations, but on open, direct and trusting responses like those of a child.

- This is a familiar theme in Jesus' teaching – that those who think they should be first shall be last, and those who are last and have humility are first to enter the Kingdom.

COST OF DISCIPLESHIP

The most important Christian quality is love. The Greek term often employed by the New Testament writers is *agape*. Agape, in its Christian context, means 'selfless love for others'. Jesus was not the only rabbi to suggest that love of God and neighbour was the basis on which the whole of the Torah was based. By love he meant not only loyalty but generous love, the kind of love which involves risking your life for others.

The cost of discipleship involves loyalty, losing one's attachment to material things, service to others and suffering.

Martyrdom: the cost of discipleship?

Dietrich Bonhoeffer

'Christians in Germany will face the terrible alternative of either willing the defeat of their nation in order that Christian civilisation may survive, or willing the victory of their nation and thereby destroying our own civilisation. I know which of these alternatives I must choose; but I cannot make that choice in security.'

Dietrich Bonhoeffer (1906–45) felt that Christians had lost the real sense of discipleship. He was imprisoned by the Nazis and executed on the evening before the Allies liberated the concentration camp where he was imprisoned.

Is dying for what one believes in the ultimate test?

Loyalty

On one occasion (3:31–35), the crowd report that Jesus' mother and brothers are looking for him. Jesus' response is to say that his true family are those who carry out God's will. It may seem like an odd remark given the importance of the family in Christian thought. Jesus challenges his disciples to consider who their true family is. Love must go beyond loyalty and attachment to family because it demands an ultimate dedication to God.

A crowd was sitting around him, and they told him, 'Your mother and brothers are outside looking for you.'

'Who are my mother and my brothers?' he asked. Then he looked at those seated in a circle around him and said, 'Here are my mother and my brothers! Whoever does God's will is my brother and sister and mother.'

Mark 3:32–35

What does it mean to be totally loyal or committed to the Kingdom of God? James Mawdsley, who campaigned for human rights in Burma, was given to several prison sentences, including one in September 1999, and jailed for 17 years. As a committed Christian he felt that his action was the only appropriate one open to him. His father said, 'People ask me, isn't James being selfish putting us through this? Well, the regime disgusts me. They have committed murder. They have committed genocide. They torture people. There are 45 million Burmese who are living their lives in fear. James is willing to put his life on the line to raise people's awareness.'

Do you think James Mawdsley is acting as a good Christian or is he being very selfish?

James Mawdsley

Attachment to Material Things

> ### KEY QUESTION
> Does a Christian have to be poor to be a good Christian?

Jesus' conversation with the Rich Young Man (10:17–31) is designed to shock. It should be remembered that the Kingdom of God in Jewish thought would be a time of plenty. The young man believes that as he has kept all the religious laws he will be rewarded with eternal life. Perhaps he believes, like many members of Jewish society at that time, that his wealth is a sign of God's reward for living a good life. Jesus' challenge that he should give up his wealth if he is to enter the Kingdom of God must have come as a considerable shock to him.

> But Jesus said again, 'Children, how hard it is to enter the Kingdom of God! It is easier for a camel to go through the eye of a needle than for a rich man to enter the Kingdom of God.'
>
> *Mark 10:24–25*

- Jesus' teaching reverses this traditional expectation. His suggestion is that it will be the poor who enter the Kingdom. In Jewish thought at the time, the poor represented all those who had been abandoned by God, so Jesus deliberately turns traditional teaching upside down.

- However, Jesus didn't necessarily mean poor in the literal sense, for there is no reason why a poor person should be any better than a rich person. 'Poor' is taken to mean the person who is not attached to his wealth or to the superficial rewards of the world.

- The reaction of the disciples (10:26) rightly recognises that this is an impossible ideal, because we are all attached to our possessions in some way. But they have forgotten that God's grace or love makes the Kingdom possible and not just human effort.

- There is much debate about what the 'eye of the needle' refers to. Some suggest that it is a narrow gate in Jerusalem where an overburdened camel would have to remove its load to pass through into Jerusalem. Others think that 'camel' should be translated as 'rope' (as the Greek words are similar), but the story gains nothing by reading it this way. Perhaps it was just Jesus' way of making his point by using an absurd metaphor to make the point that wealth makes it impossible to enter the Kingdom of God.

An absurd idea!

After his conversation with the young man, Jesus makes it clear to his shocked disciples that the Kingdom of God will offer a different kind of reward that will be 100 times more valuable (10:29–31) than any amount of wealth. It is not clear what this might be – but it could be sharing a life of love and commitment with other Christians, being a member of the Church. But the ultimate reward is not in the present world but eternal life in the age to come.

Service and Suffering

> KEY QUESTION
>
> How can a Church community be run effectively if everyone is considered equal?

It is no coincidence that Mark places one of Jesus' major teachings on lifestyle at the time when Jesus first explains his role as the suffering servant at Caesarea Philippi (8:34–38). Jesus says that if anyone wants to be a Christian he must 'deny himself and take up his cross' (8:34). Luke tones down Mark by adding 'take up one's cross *daily*' as a symbol of constant service, but as we have already seen, and as Mark spells out in Chapter 13 (see Unit 1, pages 6–7), Mark considers that self-sacrifice and suffering are to be taken literally. That is why Simon of Cyrene is an important figure at Jesus' crucifixion (15:21) because it is he who actually carries Jesus' cross when Jesus is physically too exhausted to bear it himself.

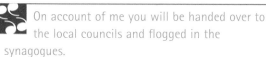

On account of me you will be handed over to the local councils and flogged in the synagogues.

Mark 13:9

A constant theme in Mark, and a characteristic of the Kingdom, is that the first will be last and the last will be first. It is a radical reversal of human expectation. The life of service is therefore a characteristic Christian virtue. This need not be in the obvious vocations of a teacher, priest, doctor, police officer and so on, but in *every* walk of life. Integrity and concern for others are not limited to certain jobs. The challenge to the Rich Young Man was a test of his genuine commitment to others. He was unable to share what he had with others and so by Jesus' standards he had not fulfilled the spirit of the Law.

Is it right for Christians to play the lottery?

A very important passage in Mark describes when James and John ask to sit on Jesus' right and left sides (10:35–45) when the new Kingdom arrives. Mark gives this great emphasis in his gospel and it probably reflects the tensions in his own community. James and John have understood Christian leadership purely in terms of reward. Perhaps they still imagined a political Kingdom rather than a spiritual or moral life. In the story, the other disciples are 'indignant' or embarrassed by James and John. But are they really any better? Jesus' final words (10:42–44) are aimed at them *all*. There have always been such problems in Church communities where there are those who think they are more important than others.

> Jesus called them together and said, 'You know that those who are regarded as rulers of the Gentiles lord it over them, and their high officials exercise authority over them. Not so with you. Instead, whoever wants to become great among you must be your servant, and whoever wants to be first must be slave of all.'
>
> *Mark 10:42–44*

TASK BOX

a) Describe some of the sacrifices that a Christian will have to make to be a member of the Church.

b) Explain the relationship in Christian terms between reward and service.

c) Discuss whether Jesus really considered the family to be less important than commitment to the Kingdom of God.

TEST YOURSELF

1 Name five of Jesus' 12 disciples.
2 Which of Jesus' disciples may have belonged to the Zealot movement?
3 What kind of person should a disciple become like in order to enter the Kingdom of God?
4 Who are Jesus' true family?
5 What was the standard Jewish teaching on wealth in Jesus' time?
6 What challenge did Jesus set the young man who had kept all the commandments?
7 Who carried Jesus' cross at his crucifixion?
8 What had James and John requested of Jesus, which embarrassed the other disciples?
9 What was Jesus' teaching on greatness and leadership?

The challenges of discipleship

The challenges of discipleship involve belief and prayer, sacrifice and reward, commitment and leadership.

Belief and Prayer

KEY QUESTION

Does Mark think Jesus' disciples are failures?

Before faith comes 'belief' – that is, the realisation of the truth and reality of God and the Kingdom. Jesus required belief first (1:15) in his preaching that the Kingdom of God was 'near'. Faith is a commitment and trust. The disciples lacked it during the Storm (4:40) on the Sea of Galilee. Lack of belief was described in the parable of the Sower and Seed as those whose commitment withered under persecution, hardship and love of material things.

Faith is closely linked with the healing miracles Jesus performed. As we have seen, Jesus' healings were not cures of the body but also the whole person. Without faith there can be no hope that a life can be changed. That is why faith can achieve extraordinary things. As Jesus said, faith can move mountains (11:22–24).

> Therefore I tell you, whatever you ask for in prayer, believe that you have received it, and it will be yours. And when you stand praying, if you hold anything against anyone, forgive him, so that your Father in heaven may forgive you your sins.'
>
> *Mark 11:24–25*

PERSPECTIVES

Traditionally there are four different types of prayer used in the Church: adoration, confession, thanksgiving and supplication. They are often remembered by the abbreviation ACTS:

Adoration. Prayers of adoration appreciate the wonder and beauty of the world that God has created. Adoration prayers often recognise how small we are in such an intricate and complex universe.

Confession. Confessional prayers are times when a person places himself or herself in the presence of God by meditating, reflecting or confessing to God. In the Garden of Gethsemane (Mark 14:35-36), Jesus prays for God's guidance. He addresses God in a very intimate and personal way as 'Abba' or Daddy. Personal prayers seek to understand the will of God for us as individuals.

Thanksgiving. Thanksgiving prayers are a means of thanking God and showing how an individual or members of the Church appreciate God's loving-kindness, for our health, family, friends and prosperity.

Supplication. Prayers of supplication fall into two kinds. Petitionary prayers ask God to aid humans in the struggle for good. They might ask for someone who is sick to be relieved of their suffering or for there to be peace in a place where there is conflict. Intercessionary prayers are when we attempt to place ourselves in the situation of others and pray for God to provide for their needs.

Do we only pray when we are worried or need something?

One indication of true faith is prayer. Prayer is not necessarily formal prayer in a church or a synagogue. Jesus often left his disciples and the crowds to pray alone (6:45–46). Prayer is an extension of faith and is the life lived in the presence of God.

The disciples failed to cure a Boy with Evil Spirits (9:14–29) because they lacked genuine faith and prayer. They had assumed that exorcising evil spirits was simply a question of saying the right words or actions. Prayer is, therefore, not only communication with God but also an attitude to others that puts forgiveness first.

Sacrifice and Reward

The story of the Widow in the Temple Treasury (12:41–44) uses a member of society who would have been the least likely example of the truly religious life. In the first century, widows, like children, had no legal status and without a husband would have had to rely on the generosity of their children. They were often poor. Mark has clearly chosen this story as a warning against the

THE WIDOWS MITES.

false commitment of the religious leaders whom Jesus accuses (12:40) of squandering the property of widows. The leaders would probably have gained the trust of widows and encouraged them to make them guardians of their property, which they then sold and kept the profits themselves.

The story tells how the widow puts her two small copper coins into the Temple Treasury. Each coin or 'lepton' (sometimes referred to as a mite) was the smallest currency in Palestine at the time, and together they were worth about one sixty-fourth of a labourer's daily pay – a minute amount of money! In contrast to the religious leaders, who had a great deal more to give, her offering was worth considerably more. Jesus points this out to his disciples because he really wants them to see an action that involves true devotion and sacrifice.

Commitment and Leadership

Does Mark dislike the disciples? We have already seen that Mark may have taken an ironic view of the titles that Jesus gave to his disciples (3:13–19). The climax comes in Mark 14 when Jesus' prediction, first given at Caesarea Philippi (8:34–38), that they would desert and betray him comes true and all the disciples desert him.

Perhaps Mark emphasised the failure of the disciples, by showing that even Jesus' closest companions were weak under persecution, to encourage his own readers. Maybe he wanted to show that the demands of the gospel are more than most humans can manage; perhaps he wanted to contrast their weakness with their subsequent recovery of faith after the crucifixion.

Most importantly, Mark focuses on Peter's denial (14:66–72). Peter, Jesus' closest disciple and the one who most strongly says that he won't leave, then does so. But at the resurrection he is forgiven and reinstated when the women at the empty tomb are told that the risen Jesus will meet the disciples *and* Peter in Galilee (16:7). In the early Church, Peter was regarded as the 'rock' (which is the literal meaning of his name) on which the Church was founded.

Peter denies knowing Jesus. Explain the reactions of the people in this picture. Was Peter a bad disciple?

TASK BOX

Read Mark 8:32–33;
9:14–19; 14:27–42;
14:66–72.
a) Summarise each passage in a couple of sentences.
b) 'Mark thinks the disciples are failures.'
Do you agree? Give reasons for your answer.

TEST YOURSELF

1 What did Jesus teach about true prayer?
2 Explain why the disciples couldn't cure the Boy with Evil Spirits.
3 Outline the story of the Widow in the Temple Treasury.
4 What did Jesus say to Peter at Caesarea Philippi after he predicted his suffering and death?
5 What does 'Peter' mean literally?

1 a. Who was Levi? [2]
b. Describe what happened when Jesus' family came to ask for him. [6]
c. Explain why discipleship involves sacrifice, according to Mark. [8]
d. 'To be a Christian means giving up all one's wealth.'
Do you agree? Give reasons for your opinion, showing you have considered another point of view. In your answer you should refer to Mark's Gospel. [4]

2 Mark 14:27–31

'You will all fall away,' Jesus told them, 'for it is written: "I will strike the shepherd, and the sheep will be scattered." But after I have risen, I will go ahead of you into Galilee.' Peter declared, 'Even if all fall away, I will not.' 'I tell you the truth,' Jesus answered, 'today—yes, tonight—before the cock crows twice you yourself will disown me three times.' But Peter insisted emphatically, 'Even if I have to die with you, I will never disown you.' And all the others said the same.

a. Explain what is meant by:
(i) 'I will strike the shepherd';
(ii) 'and the sheep will be scattered'. [2]
b. Outline the occasion when Jesus' warning to Peter came true. [4]
c. What did Jesus teach about the cost of being a disciple? [4]
d. 'Jesus expected far too much of his disciples. Christians today cannot possibly make such sacrifices.'
Do you agree? Give reasons for your answer, showing that you have thought about more than one point of view. [5]

Assignment

WEBLINKS

- The life of Dietrich Bonhoeffer: www.ushmm.org/bonhoeffer
- James Mawdsley's campaign for human rights: www.freedom-now.org/mawd.php
- The missionary work of USPG: www.uspg.org.uk
- Emmaus communities for the homeless: www.emmaus.org.uk
- Trinity Hospice for the sick and dying: www.trinityhospice.org.uk/
- Council for World Mission: www.cwmission.org.uk/
- Corrymeela work on prejudice: www.corrymeela.org/

REMEMBER

- **Discipleship means being a follower of Jesus' teaching and example.**
- **Being a disciple is not a job but a vocation.**
- **Being a disciple means working with others to create a community.**
- **Creating a Christian community (or church) is the way in which the Kingdom of God is established on earth.**

6

KEY WORDS

Oral law: The oral interpretation of the written law of Moses (the Torah), which the Pharisees followed because they thought it would make them holy.

Pharisees: Those who were not priests but who believed that by keeping to the oral law they would receive reward in the afterlife.

Priests: Those who, through birth, assisted in the Temple in Jerusalem. The senior priests or 'chief priests' assisted the High Priest.

Sadducees: These came largely from senior Jerusalem priestly families. They did not believe in the oral law or life after death.

Teachers of the law or scribes: These were Israel's civil servants. Many assisted in the Temple law court.

Torah or written law: This was given to Moses at Mount Sinai and contained 613 commandments covering every aspect of life. Found in the first books of the Old Testament or Hebrew Bible.

Tradition: Another term used by Mark to refer to the oral law, or the customs of worship passed by the Pharisees but not ones necessarily found in the Torah.

As we saw in Unit 5, the early Christians called themselves members of 'The Way'. The members of The Way had to struggle to find their new identity, at first within Judaism. As time went on, members of The Way left Judaism and established their own religious way of life. Only then did they think of themselves as Christians. Mark's Gospel not only records the struggle Jesus had with the Jewish authorities, but (as we have seen in Unit 1) reflects the conflicts and challenges Mark was going through when he wrote his gospel.

This unit looks at Jesus' challenge to authority, his challenge to religious traditions and to worship.

CHALLENGE TO AUTHORITY

Mark's Gospel is carefully arranged so that after the first two glorious 'days' (Chapter 1) he contrasts the joy of the Kingdom with its struggle against the prejudice of society and its traditions. The **teachers of the law** and **Pharisees** (laymen) in these stories are really stereotypes, and represent all those in a society who put their laws before ethics and their traditions before people. The Pharisees were not bad people, but they felt an

obligation to make sure that all the traditions of their ancestors and their interpretation of the laws were kept so that Israel could truly become a holy nation. The disputes between them and Jesus are not over the basics of the **Torah** but about the lawyers' and Pharisees' interpretation of the law. Eventually, their disagreements led to Jesus' death.

A Pharisee wearing a prayer shawl and phylacteries on his arm and forehead.

Conflict and the challenge of ideas and lifestyle still continue to be a feature of Christian life today.

The following passages come from a section in Mark where he has collected five conflict stories (2:1–3:6) that illustrate Jesus' teaching on forgiveness of sins, religious rules about fasting and the principle of having a day of rest.

Authority to Forgive Sins (2:1–12)

KEY QUESTION

Is curing someone easier than forgiving their sins?

In this story of the Paralysed Man, the four friends of the paralysed man have to dig their way through the flat roof of the house where Jesus is teaching because the crowd makes it impossible for them to get to the door. Although Jesus recognises the friends' faith (rather than the faith of the ill man), he uses the occasion to challenge the teachers of the law about whether human forgiveness of sins is against God's will.

Instead of immediately curing the man he says, 'Son, your sins are forgiven' (2:5). This was an intentionally provocative remark:

- According to the Jewish teaching, only God could remove a person's sins.
- Jesus was making a point that if in Jewish thought physical illness was considered to be the punishment for the man's or even his parents' sins, then curing the body is the *same* as forgiveness of sins.
- Jesus' challenge is not only to point out the inconsistency in Jewish thought but to show that true forgiveness must be of the *whole* person, their soul and body.

The question Jesus asks is a challenging one still: which is easier – to heal someone or to forgive them? Both might be equally difficult depending on the circumstance.

> Which is easier: to say to the paralytic, 'Your sins are forgiven,' or to say, 'Get up, take your mat and walk'?
>
> *Mark 2:9*

The Paralysed Man was lowered through the roof by his friends because of the crowds by the door. Jesus' cure caused an angry debate with the teachers of the law. Why?

Jesus goes on to say that as Son of Man (see Unit 8, page 110–11) he is God's representative and therefore has the authority to take away sins.

In traditional Christian thought, although it is a Christian duty to forgive other people, only the Church as a representative of God on earth has the authority to absolve sin. In a church service where the priest gives absolution, it is not he as an individual who removes sin, but his words as a special (or ordained) representative of the Church. This is not an easy idea, and the meaning of the story of the Paralysed Man has always been the subject of a great deal of debate.

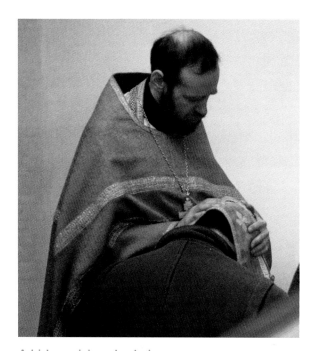

A bishop giving absolution.

Fasting (2:18–22)

KEY QUESTION

Are there any good religious reasons why Christians should sometimes fast?

Jesus was reprimanded because he was not keeping to the special fast days on Tuesdays and Thursdays, which the followers of the Pharisees stuck to. The debate is not really about fasting but the reasons why Judaism is no longer the basis of authority for Christianity. Again the conversation is not easy, but it can be summarised in this way:

- If one was a guest of the bridegroom at a wedding then it would be quite wrong to fast if the wedding happened to be on a Tuesday or a Thursday, as this would spoil the purpose of being at the wedding festivities.
- So, as Jesus is the bridegroom, then his disciples do not need to fast.
- If Christians choose to fast after Jesus has died, their reason for doing so is not based on Jewish authority but to remember Jesus' life and teaching.
- Therefore, Christians should see that their authority comes from the new teaching of Jesus on the Kingdom. Any attempt to combine the old authority of Jewish custom is like putting new wine into old wineskins (new wine causes old leather to split), or a new unshrunk piece of cloth onto old cloth. In both cases the new will destroy the old.

A modern wineskin.

No-one pours new wine into old wineskins. If he does, the wine will burst the skins, and both the wine and the wineskins will be ruined. No, he pours new wine into new wineskins.

Mark 2:22

Challenge to the Sabbath Laws

KEY QUESTION

What are the most important moral values for society?

All the gospels record Jesus' conflicts with the authorities over the Sabbath. The Sabbath is the weekly reminder of God's covenant through the creation (God rested on the seventh day) and the Torah ('keep the Sabbath day holy'). The Sabbath gave Israel her identity and was a basis for social justice in so far as it prohibited masters from making their servants work every day of the week.

Plucking the Corn on the Sabbath (2:23–28)

Mark imagines that as Jesus' disciples are walking through the cornfields on the Sabbath, they are plucking and possibly rubbing the corn to make flour. According to the Torah, it is illegal to work on the Sabbath (Deuteronomy 23:25) and what Jesus and his disciples have done is considered to be work. Jesus' response places human need above the **traditions** of the Sabbath. By referring to David – when he and his companions were hungry, he ate the holy bread in the Temple that only the priests could eat – his accusers realise that even the great king of Israel wasn't bound by human tradition when this special situation arose. Preservation of life is a fundamental principle of the Torah. 'The Sabbath was made for man' was a saying well known to other rabbis, which Jesus reinforced.

Cornfields in Galilee today. Even an innocent walk in the cornfields on the Sabbath caused a row with the Pharisees. Were they right to criticise Jesus for breaking the Sabbath rules?

Sunday as a day of worship

Why is Sunday a day of rest for Christians? The Ten Commandments state that on the seventh day of the week humans should cease work (Exodus 20:8) as a reminder that after the sixth day God completed the creation. The time therefore is for re-creation, time free from weekly work. It is also a time for worship and to thank God for his creation. Christians changed their Sabbath from the Saturday to the Sunday because this is the day when the women got to the tomb where Jesus was buried to find that he had been resurrected (Mark 16:1–2). Sunday therefore is also a celebration of the Resurrection. Modern lifestyle often makes keeping Sunday special very difficult, and many, Christians included, would like Sunday to return to being a day of rest. Some argue that without a day of rest people can become overworked and exploited. The Sunday question is, therefore, a debate about the value society places on people and the freedom for people to choose how they wish to live their lives.

Healing a Man with a Shrivelled Hand (3:1–6)

The issue is not whether the Sabbath should be kept but how it should be kept. The Pharisees allowed for life-threatening cases to be cured on the Sabbath. The issue is whether the man's illness is fatal. Clearly it is not. But Jesus' response is that *all* life is sacred and that this situation demands a cure; there are times when we should not put people's needs off until tomorrow. Mark contrasts Jesus' desire to cure the man, with the Pharisees' wish to kill him (3:6)! Jesus concludes that God gave people the Sabbath to be a time of rest; human Sabbath laws should carry out God's intentions and not make life more difficult and stressful.

The Sabbath was made for man, not man for the Sabbath. So the Son of Man is Lord even of the Sabbath.

Mark 2:27–28

TEST YOURSELF

1 What did the Pharisees believe?
2 Why was Jesus criticised for curing the paralysed man?
3 What parable did Jesus tell to justify breaking the fast day?
4 What does the Sabbath remember?
5 What does Sunday remember for Christians today?
6 What reason did Jesus give for plucking corn on the Sabbath?

a) Tell the story of the Paralysed Man from the point of view of one of the lawyers who debated with Jesus.
b) Explain the relationship between sin and illness in Jesus' time.
c) Explain the significance of Jesus' parable of the old and new wine skins and the old cloth and new patch.
d) Prepare notes for a class debate: 'The law should make it possible for everyone to have the same day of rest each week.' Think which side of the debate you will be supporting.

KEY QUESTION

What really matters in religion?

The theme of the passages in Mark 7:1–23 and 10:1–12 is that holiness and true moral behaviour come from a person's attitude, or what some have called the inner law. Jesus' teaching is critical of those who follow any tradition without thinking and who therefore often disregard the needs of others. His main criticism is of those who use tradition to evade their own responsibilities.

ing to these laws cannot in themselves make a person good or holy. Worship and ritual cleanness of any kind in church or at home is empty unless it is accompanied by a pure heart and good intentions. Ritual cleanness is another way of referring to the religious ceremonies and customs that lead to spiritual purity, not necessarily actual physical cleanness.

'These people honour me with their lips, but their hearts are far from me.'

Mark 7:7

Jesus quotes from Isaiah 29:13.

TASK BOX

a) What is a 'tradition'?
b) Give some examples of traditions in our own society or in your family.
c) Explain why some people think traditions are important in society.
d) Discuss: 'The Church should get rid of its ancient traditions if it is to appeal to twenty-first-century people'.

Corban (7:9–13)

Mark gives another example where the **oral law** has become more important than the Torah, or where religious extremism has cancelled out true morality. Corban means literally 'offered to God'. Originally it meant a sacrifice or 'offering to God'. Jesus uses corban as an example where a person could say that they had carried out their religious duties by giving money to the Temple and thereby argue that they had no need to give money to their parents, even though one of the Ten Commandments stated that they should 'honour their mother and father' (Exodus 20:12). Jesus' warning is against those who have become so clever with their religious argument that they have forgotten what really matters. He warns that it is very easy to become hypocritical.

Hand Washing (7:1–8)

The washing of hands was not originally a general custom but one that applied only to the priests when they ate holy food.

The Pharisees seem to have adopted the custom for themselves and imposed this extreme law on their ordinary members. They hoped in this way to become holy. But Jesus' criticism is that keep-

You have a fine way of setting aside the commandments of God in order to observe your own traditions!

Mark 7:9

Food Laws (7:14–23)

This is quite a shocking verse. Food or kosher laws for a Jew were a matter of some importance and were part of his or her religious duty and identity, such as keeping milk and meat separate and not eating pork. Once again, it is possible that Jesus taught that it is the intention behind the laws that is important, not just keeping laws for their own sake. Jesus gives a list of sins (for example sexual immorality, theft, murder and greed) so that his listeners understand that food cannot cause sin (it simply passes through the body), only bad intentions can cause sin.

It is more than likely that Mark added the final comment 'making all foods clean' (7:19) to suggest that keeping to kosher laws was no longer necessary for Christians. It must have been very hard for many Jews who had converted to Christianity in Mark's community to have accepted this teaching at first.

> Nothing outside a man can make him 'unclean' by going into him. Rather, it is what comes out of a man that makes him 'unclean'.
>
> *Mark 7:25*

Food laws are still very important in modern Judaism. Did Jesus mean to abolish all kosher laws?

Divorce (10:1–12)

The emphasis of Jesus' teaching here is on divorce and not marriage, because at the time various Jewish rabbis had been debating on what grounds a divorce could take place.

■ Rabbi Hillel (a liberal) argued divorce could be for anything that displeased the husband.

■ Rabbi Shammai (a conservative) argued divorce could only be on grounds of adultery.

■ Jesus' argument is to remind them what the basic religious rules are for marriage. Marriage is a religious covenant or promise between a man and a woman which makes them 'one flesh' (10:8). Once made it cannot be broken (10:9); that was what God intended from the beginning of creation (10:6).

You will notice, however, that in 10:10–12 Jesus does appear to allow for some kind of divorce. There is much debate over what he meant here. One interpretation is that Jesus allowed separation but banned re-marriage. Re-marriage is considered as equivalent to adultery (10:11) because the original couple(s) are still married in the eyes of God. The heart of Jesus' teaching, is that true marriage is not just about going through a wedding ceremony, but is a life-long commitment.

A modern Jewish wedding under a huppah.

The question of re-marriage is still much debated by Christians today. The Roman Catholic Church argues that there can be no divorce, only 'annulment', or the acknowledgement that for various reasons the marriage vows were never fulfilled and so a couple may separate. Most Protestants, on the other hand, consider that there can be divorce. Some argue that there can be no re-marriage, but others consider that there can be re-marriage when a marriage has failed and where the new couple fully intend to make a new relationship. This is because the heart of Jesus' teaching is based on repentance, forgiveness and commitment.

ISSUES IN HUMAN SEXUALITY

A Statement by the House of Bishops

The issue of divorce and re-marriage is much debated today in the Church.

TEST YOURSELF

1 What is meant by the 'inner law'?
2 Give an example of Jewish ritual cleanness.
3 What does 'corban' mean?
4 Why did Jesus use the example of corban to criticise the Pharisees and teachers of the law?
5 Give an example of Jewish kosher food laws.
6 What did Jesus teach on the subject of food laws?
7 What did Jesus say was the original purpose of marriage?
8 What did Jesus teach about divorce?
9 What was Jesus' teaching on re-marriage?

WHY DID JESUS CHALLENGE THE INSTITUTION OF THE TEMPLE?

KEY QUESTION

What did Jesus think about the role of the Temple in Jewish religious life?

The Temple was the symbol of Israel's religious and political authority. It was first built by King Solomon (960 BCE), and after it was destroyed in 586 BCE by the Babylonians, it was rebuilt but on a much smaller scale. Finally, Herod the Great (37–4 BCE) built the third and last temple on a grand scale. It was this Temple that Jesus visited and which was still being completed during his lifetime. It was destroyed in 70 CE by the Romans and has never been rebuilt.

Like many prophets before him, Jesus' treatment of the Temple symbolised his attitude to the state of Israel's religion and politics *and* to the guardians of the Temple – the **priests**, chief priests and the High Priest. In some Jewish teachings, the age to come or the Kingdom of God would only arrive when the messiah had made sure that the Temple was pure and clean. In other traditions, the Temple would be destroyed and a new, perfect and heavenly Temple would be given by God from heaven.

Jesus' Predictions about his Death and Resurrection

Jesus spoke ambiguously about the Temple. In Mark 13:1–2 he said to his disciples, as they sat on the Mount of Olives overlooking the Temple, that the Temple would be destroyed by others. But at his trial (14:57–59) his accusers thought he had said that *he* would destroy the Temple and then magically create a new one after three days. They had probably misheard Jesus predicting the end of ancient Judaism when he spoke of

The Western Wall in Jerusalem today. The last remains of the Temple. The temple symbolised God's presence on earth. Why was it so important in Jesus' teaching?

his death and resurrection (9:31–32). He may even have meant that his body was to symbolise the Temple, and his resurrection with the new body of believers was to symbolise the Church. Whatever Jesus may have said, his accusers at his trial certainly considered his attack on the Temple to have been a major reason for putting him to death.

> 'The Son of Man is going to be betrayed into the hands of men. They will kill him, and after three days he will rise.' But they did not understand what he meant and were afraid to ask him about it.
>
> *Mark 9:31–32*
>
> So important is this part of Jesus' teaching that Mark records Jesus' predictions of his future suffering three times (Mark 8:31, 9:31–32 and 10:32–34).

Jesus' Triumphal Entry into Jerusalem and the Cleansing of the Temple show his desire for a radical reform of religion and explain why the authorities were provoked into plotting his downfall.

Triumphal Entry into Jerusalem (11:1–11)

The Cleansing of the Temple is part of a single story which includes the Triumphal Entry. It is typical of Mark to break up the story with the incident of the Cursing of the Fig Tree. All three moments are challenges to the chief priests as guardians of Judaism.

- Jesus' action is typical of the Old Testament prophets who often acted out symbols. The first stage is to prepare his disciples by getting them to collect a colt from the village (11:2–6).

Jesus' triumphal entry into Jerusalem. Today this is celebrated by Christians as Palm Sunday. Why is this an important festival in the Church's year?

- The colt is religiously pure because it has never been ridden (11:2). It symbolises the purity of the new Kingdom which the people think Jesus will establish (the Old Testament predicted that the messiah, the Son of King David, would establish this Kingdom, 11:10). But it is more likely that Jesus thought he was fulfilling the prophecy of Zechariah (9:9) that the messiah would come as a humble, peaceful figure, not a military, kingly figure riding on horseback.

> See your king comes to you, righteous and riding on a donkey, on a colt, the foal of a donkey ... He will proclaim peace to all the nations.
>
> *Zechariah 9:9–10*

- As Jesus enters Jerusalem the people shout out *hosanna* (11:9) as they recite part of Psalm 118, which looked forward to the coming of the messiah. *Hosanna* means 'save'.

They are looking for God to save his people and bring in his Kingdom.

- In Psalm 118 there is mention of waving of branches (11:8) to rejoice in the coming of God. In John's Gospel these are described as palm branches, which is why this event is often known as Palm Sunday in the Christian year.

Cleansing the Temple (11:12–21)

KEY QUESTION

How did the cleansing of the Temple lead to the plot to have Jesus killed?

On his way to the Temple Jesus performs a very strange action – he curses a fig tree that hadn't any fruit. The following day, after he has cleansed the Temple, he returned to find that the tree had completely withered and died. The Cursing of the Fig Tree (11:12–14 and 20–21) is a difficult story to interpret, however it makes sense to see it as a

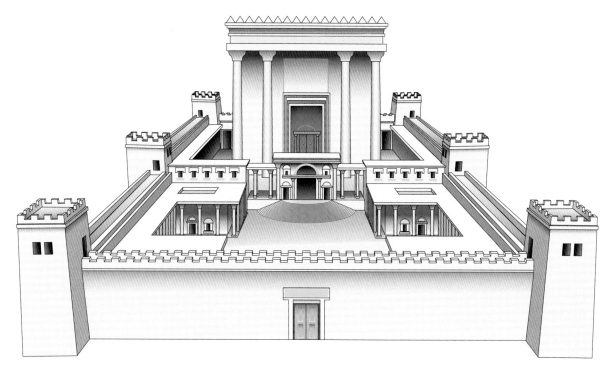

Herod the Great's Temple at the time of Jesus. The central tower contained the ark of the Covenant and was the most holy place in the temple, which only the High Priest could enter. The traders and money lenders had probably set up their stalls outside these walls.

Jesus cleanses the Temple. Was Jesus angry or disappointed with the traders of the Temple authorities?

private symbolic action to prepare the disciples for his action in the Temple. Did Jesus actually kill the fig tree? It is very difficult to know what actually happened. Some people argue that it was dying anyway and that Jesus used it as means of teaching. Others think he told a parable of the cursing of a fig tree that has been misremembered.

- The fig tree (11:13) represents the Jewish leaders.
- Mark explains that the tree has no fruit because it was not the season (11:13). The Jewish leaders have failed to produce fruit or good works because they have misjudged the situation.
- Jesus' curse, 'May no one eat fruit from you again' (11:14), is typical of the Old Testament prophets who passed God's judgement on those who had failed to live religious lives.
- The general warning is a judgement on those superior people who think that they don't have to do good works because of their position in society.

The Cleansing of the Temple (11:15–19) is the fulfilment of the Jewish idea that the messiah, or the new age, would only arrive once the Temple had been cleansed and made pure. There was no agreement whether Gentiles would be included or not.

> In the last days the mountain of the LORD's temple will be established as chief among the mountains; it will be raised above the hills, and peoples will stream to it. Many nations will come and say, 'Come, let us go up to the mountain of the LORD, to the house of the God of Jacob. He will teach us his ways, so that we may walk in his paths.'
>
> *Micah 4:1–2*

- When Jesus says that the Temple should be a 'House for all nations' he is perhaps suggesting that the Kingdom of God is to include Gentiles and all those whom the priests would reject as being unsuitable.

> 'Is it not written: "My house will be called a house of prayer for all nations"? But you have made it a "den of robbers".'

Mark 11:17

Jesus quotes both the prophets Isaiah and Jeremiah to justify his action in the Temple.

TASK BOX

a) Find out about and describe the main moments of the Christian celebration called Holy Week.

b) What did Jesus hope to achieve by throwing out the traders in the Temple?

c) 'Jesus' attitude to the Temple suggests that there should be no organised religion today.' Do you agree? Give reasons for your answer.

- The selling of doves (11:15) was for pilgrims to offer them up as a symbol of their prayers. The money-changer (11:15) was allowed to change non-Temple money into Temple money. Probably Jesus' criticism is that the process has become corrupt ('den of robbers') and the pilgrims are being exploited by being overcharged.

- Jesus also forbids them even to carry merchandise (11:16) through the Temple. Perhaps the Temple was being used as a short cut. Jesus' exaggerated action makes the point that the Temple should be the place where God is remembered.

- Jesus' action causes the chief priests to plot to kill him (11:18). This is an extreme reaction. But Mark makes it clear that Jesus' action and words are understood to be critical of official Judaism. Jesus' action is reported to the priests and their legal advisors. They understand its implications immediately. They realise that Jesus is not only challenging their authority as religious leaders but their characters are being judged as well.

> The chief priests and the teachers of the law heard this and began looking for a way to kill him, for they feared him, because the whole crowd was amazed at his teaching.

Mark 11:18

WHAT ARE THE ARGUMENTS THAT LED TO JESUS' BETRAYAL?

The final set of debates that Mark includes are all set in the Temple outer courts (probably not in the Temple itself) where Jesus debates a series of technical questions with various members of the Jewish authorities. Each argument shows the weaknesses of their religious beliefs and at the same time gives them further reasons for disliking Jesus' presence in Jerusalem.

Authority and Conflict (11:27–33)

> Jesus replied, 'I will ask you one question. Answer me, and I will tell you by what authority I am doing these things. John's baptism—was it from heaven, or from men? Tell me!' They discussed it among themselves and said, 'If we say, "From heaven", he will ask, "Then why didn't you believe him?" But if we say, "From men" . . .' (They feared the people, for everyone held that John really was a prophet.) So they answered Jesus, 'We don't know.' Jesus said, 'Neither will I tell you by what authority I am doing these things.'

Mark 11:29–33

This episode gives several reasons why the authorities want Jesus removed. Quite reasonably they ask by what authority Jesus acts when he cleansed the Temple. This was a difficult question because the answer can only be 'by the authority of God'. Jesus' answer is of course that he is acting under God's authority, but by Jewish law he would have to find some reliable witnesses to back up his claim. He could point to his miracles or to other teachers or prophets. So, he chooses the witness of John the Baptist (11:30).

Perhaps Jesus knows that whatever witness he chooses they will probably find fault. But his choice of John emphasises that his water baptism was a preparation for his own baptism with the Holy Spirit (1:8). If the Jewish authorities recognise that John the Baptist's baptism was from God then they would logically also have to accept Jesus' authority. But for whatever reasons they are unable to accept that John is a prophet sent by God.

The authorities are therefore left in the humiliating position of having to show their ignorance and concluding that they 'don't know' (11:33) the answer to Jesus' question. By placing them in this awkward position, Jesus antagonises them more and increases their desire to have him removed.

Paying taxes to Caesar (12:13–17)

A denarius showing Caesar's head.

Jesus said to them, 'Give to Caesar what is Caesar's and to God what is God's.'

Mark 12:17

KEY QUESTION

Is a Christian justified in breaking the law of the land if it conflicts with his or her beliefs?

Paying taxes was, and still is, a sensitive issue. The reference to the Herodians (12:12) suggests that these particular Pharisees might have been more pro-Rome than some others. Their question is intended to catch Jesus out, although the question of loyalty to Rome was hotly debated amongst the leaders of Judaism at the time. The real objection was not that tax had to be paid, but that they couldn't rule themselves as they were under the ultimate non-Jewish power of Caesar. Their question, 'Is it right to pay taxes to Caesar or not?' (12:14) is intended to be unanswerable.

Clearly if Jesus tells them to worship God, it is in effect licence to ignore Rome, which would be treacherous. On the other hand, loyalty to Rome through paying taxes would be equivalent to blasphemy.

The coin or denarius Jesus requests (12:15) would not have been Temple money (and technically useless in the Temple) as it had Caesar's portrait or head (12:16) on it. However, the fact that Roman money is being used at all suggests that loyalty to the government did not necessarily mean disloyalty to God. Jesus' answer is that we should give to Caesar what is due to him and to God (12:17) what is due to him. This appears to suggest that Christians have a duty to uphold law and order as part of their religious duty. However, Christians have frequently debated whether Jesus' teaching is always appropriate. Supposing, for instance, the law is a bad law and is causing suffering or evil. Would it still be a religious duty to obey it?

Civil disobedience

In recent times, Martin Luther King Junior (1929–1968) is a good example of a Christian who acted against the law. King considered that the law in the USA that discriminated against black people was a bad law. He led a whole series of non-violent protests, beginning with a boycott of buses in Montgomery in 1955.

Arrested in 1963 by the police in Birmingham, Alabama, he led a massive peaceful protest march of 250,000 people to Washington in the same year. He often described his journey as being like Moses leading the people to the promised land, and he believed that the Kingdom of God should be inclusive of all people, whatever their race or creed. A major victory was achieved in 1964 with the passing of a new Civil Rights Act. But if, as King said, 'unjust laws are no laws at all' then the time has come to act. As he said in his famous letter from Birmingham jail, 'We know through painful experience that freedom is never voluntarily given by the oppressor; it must be demanded by the oppressed.'

King knew that his actions would place his life in danger and he was assassinated in 1968.

How can a Christian decide whether a law is just or unjust? Isn't it better for religion and politics to be kept separate?

The crowds in Washington whom King addressed on the subject of equal rights.

Resurrection (12:18–27)

KEY QUESTION

If there is an afterlife, what kind of relationships will people have with one another?

The challenge of the **Sadducees** hinges on whether Jesus' teaching on resurrection and life after death is blasphemous. The Sadducees belonged to an older tradition of Judaism that denied any idea of afterlife because there was no evidence for it in the Torah. This is not an easy story to interpret; Jesus is not just pointing out their misunderstanding of resurrection but also their method of arguing.

The Sadducees' argument begins by inventing an imaginary situation based on a law contained in the Torah called Levirate marriage (Deuteronomy 25:5–10) whereby if a woman's husband died his brother could take her as his wife even if he was married already. Polygamy (having more than one wife) was allowed in extreme circumstances. The Sadducees invent a situation whereby each of her husband's seven brothers dies and she becomes a new wife to each successive brother.

- The Sadducees' challenge is whether in heaven she would be married to all seven husbands at the same time (12:23).
- If Jesus agrees then the Sadducees will argue that she would be committing adultery seven times in heaven and that would mean that God would be contradicting himself as his law forbids adultery (Exodus 20:14).
- As God cannot contradict himself it follows, according to the Sadducees' logic, that there can be no resurrection or afterlife.

Jesus' reply is to play the Sadducees at their own game with a clever piece of biblical interpretation – even though it may not sound very convincing to us.

- Jesus argues that at the burning bush (Exodus 3:6) God tells Moses that he is the God of Abraham, Isaac and Jacob (12:26), all of whom are dead in the physical sense. However, if God is God equally of Moses as well as of the three 'dead' patriarchs they

must also be alive but not on earth. It follows that they must be living in heaven.

- Finally, Jesus is able to argue that the reason why they cannot accept the resurrection is that their idea of afterlife is too physical, whereas heaven is not a place like this world but a much more spiritual existence. Therefore, Jesus concludes: God's laws that govern marriage, adultery and divorce on earth are irrelevant in heaven (12:25). The woman with seven husbands cannot be committing adultery in heaven because she will be like an angel (12:25) or heavenly being, not an earthly, physical being.

> When the dead rise, they will neither marry nor be given in marriage; they will all live like angels in heaven.
>
> *Mark 12:25*

Jesus' teaching poses an important question about what it would be like to be resurrected. There is more discussion about Jesus' resurrection on pages 92–96.

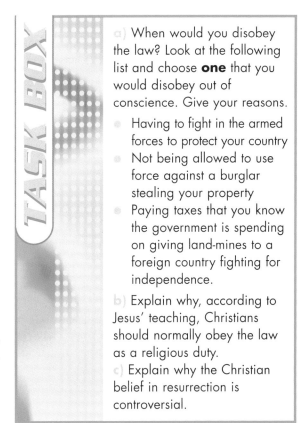

TASK BOX

a) When would you disobey the law? Look at the following list and choose **one** that you would disobey out of conscience. Give your reasons.

- Having to fight in the armed forces to protect your country
- Not being allowed to use force against a burglar stealing your property
- Paying taxes that you know the government is spending on giving land-mines to a foreign country fighting for independence.

b) Explain why, according to Jesus' teaching, Christians should normally obey the law as a religious duty.

c) Explain why the Christian belief in resurrection is controversial.

The Greatest Commandment (12:28–34)

KEY QUESTION

Is there one moral commandment all humans should obey?

There was a regular debate amongst the rabbis on whether the Torah could be summarised. According to tradition there were 613 commandments covering everything from rituals to ethical principles. The challenge to Jesus by the teacher of the law is not as hostile as the other challenges by the Jewish authorities in the Temple. In fact, Jesus' reply is very similar to the views held by many other rabbis at the time. Jesus summarises the Torah by quoting two passages from it and offering them as one principle.

> Hear O Israel: The Lord our God, the Lord is one. Love the Lord your God with all your heart and with all your soul and with all your strength.
>
> *Deuteronomy 6:4*
>
> Do not seek revenge or bear a grudge against one of your people, but love your neighbour as yourself.
>
> *Leviticus 19:18*
>
> What is hateful to yourself, do not do to your neighbour; this is the whole Law, the rest is commentary.
>
> *Rabbi Hillel, a first-century rabbi*

■ The first (12:29–30) is from Deuteronomy 6:4 and is a portion of the shema. The shema was the most important prayer in Judaism then and is still so today. It reminds the person that there is only one God who requires the loyalty of the whole person, i.e. heart (body), soul (spirit), mind (reason).

This mezuzah contains the shema and is placed on the door frame of a Jewish home. Jews and Christians share the same duty to love the one God with all their heart and mind.

■ The second passage (12:31) is from Leviticus 19:18, and urges the good Christian to love one's neighbour as one's self. The lawyer repeats back Jesus' teaching and adds that this is true religion; false religion is the one that makes the rituals and the ceremonies more important than moral and spiritual demands.
■ It is hard to know quite how radical Jesus' teaching is, because to a Jew 'neighbour' would probably have only meant his Jewish neighbour, but Jesus probably means anyone, whatever their religion or belief.

However, the story poses a problem that Christians have answered in very different ways. Did Jesus' great commandment mean that almost all the other commandments of the Torah were no longer necessary and that the only moral principle that is necessary to live a Christian life is love? Or did he mean that living life according to the laws of the Torah is the only way a person can live a loving life?

TEST YOURSELF

1 How many times did Jesus predict his death and resurrection?
2 What animal did Jesus ride into Jerusalem?
3 What did the people shout out as they waved their branches?
4 What was Jesus' curse on the fig tree?
5 Name the three things which Jesus pointed out had corrupted the Temple.
6 What had caused Jesus to say, 'Neither will I tell you by what authority I am doing these things'?
7 Why did Jesus ask for a coin to be given to him with Caesar's head on it?
8 Outline the Sadducees' example with which they hoped to prove to Jesus that there is no resurrection.
9 What did Jesus say that people became like after death in heaven?
10 What did Jesus say was the greatest commandment?

TASK BOX

a) Outline the main moments of Jesus' debates with the authorities in the Temple that led to his betrayal.
b) Read the following statements. State whether you agree or disagree with each one and give a brief reason.

- Having an abortion depends on whether it is the most loving thing to do in that situation.
- Keeping one's promises is always the most loving thing to do.
- Stealing from the rich to give to the poor is sometimes the most loving thing to do.
- It is always the most loving thing to do to be obedient to your mother and father.

c) 'Jesus taught that love is more important than being obedient to the Ten Commandments.'
Do you agree? Give reasons for your answer.

1 a. What is meant by ritual cleanness? [2]

   b. Describe how Jesus cleansed the Temple. [6]

   c. Explain why Jesus' discussion with the Sadducees about resurrection was important. [8]

   d. 'Jesus disliked all religious traditions.'

     Do you agree? Give reasons for your opinion, showing you have considered another point of view. In your answer you should refer to Mark's Gospel. [4]

2 a. Describe in detail **either**

     (i) the healing in the synagogue of the man with the evil spirit, **or**

     (ii) the healing in the synagogue of the man with the withered hand. [6]

   b. (i) Explain why the Sabbath is celebrated by Jews on the seventh day and by Christians on the first day (Sunday) of the week. [3]

     (ii) Explain why Jesus and the religious leaders disagreed about keeping the Sabbath. [6]

   c. 'Sunday is a day for worshipping God, not trading and shopping!'

     Do you agree? Give reasons for your answer, showing that you have thought about more than one point of view. [5]

Assignment

🌲 Keep Sunday special campaign: www.jubilee-centre.org/kss/

🌲 Articles from The Jubilee Centre on Christian challenges to society: www.jubilee-centre.org

🌲 Holy Week: www.cresourcei.org/cyholyweek.html

🌲 Martin Luther King Jr: go to www.westminster-abbey.org/ and use the 'Quick Search'.

🌲 Arguments about resurrection: www.riverpower.org/resurrection.htm

WEBLINKS

REMEMBER

▸ Jesus placed God's authority higher than human religious traditions.

▸ Religious beliefs will always come into conflict with some aspects of society.

▸ Jesus did not deliberately challenge the state or the law of the land, in fact he taught that Christians should be obedient to it.

▸ Jesus' basic principle, which challenges both religious and non-religious people, is whether they actually love their neighbour.

UNIT SEVEN — Suffering, Death and Resurrection

7

KEY WORDS

Blasphemy: Any act that challenges the supremacy of God. In Jewish law this could mean challenging the place of the Temple or setting one's self up to be equal with God. The High Priest charged Jesus with committing blasphemy.

Passion story: The story of Jesus' suffering or 'passion', from his anointing at Bethany until his crucifixion.

Passover: One of the three great pilgrim festivals in Judaism, which celebrates the time when the Jews were freed from slavery in Egypt and journeyed to the Promised Land.

Resurrection: The moment when, in Christian thought, the body is transformed after death and the soul and new body live on in the afterlife. This is *not* the same as reincarnation (when the soul is given a new body).

Sanhedrin or the Great Assembly: This was the senior law court in Israel, made up of 71 members. It comprised chief priests, senior members of society and scribes (or lawyers). They condemned Jesus to death for blasphemy.

Treason: Any act that undermines the authority of the government. Jesus was found guilty of being a threat to the authority of Roman rule by Pontius Pilate. The punishment was death.

THE HEART OF THE GOSPEL

At the centre of all the books and letters of the New Testament there is one unifying claim: Jesus' death and subsequent **resurrection** had created a new relationship between humans and God. This means that although we might want to know what actually happened historically, the early Christian writers were more interested in the theological meaning of the events. So, for example, the crucifixion of Jesus symbolised the wickedness to which humans can sink and the resurrection symbolised the triumph of good over evil and the promise of life after death. And to confirm this, they also saw that God's promises of the Old Testament had been fulfilled.

TASK BOX

In the following extract from Saint Paul's letter to the Corinthians, Paul summarises the key Christian beliefs.

Now, brothers, I want to remind you of the gospel I preached to you, which you received and on which you have taken your stand. By this gospel you are saved, if you hold firmly to the word I preached to you. Otherwise, you have believed in vain. For what I received I passed on to you as of first importance: that Christ died for our sins according to the Scriptures, that he was buried, that he was raised on the third day according to the Scriptures, and that he appeared to Peter, and then to the Twelve ...

But if it is preached that Christ has been raised from the dead, how can some of you say that there is no resurrection of the dead? If there is no resurrection of the dead, then not even Christ has been raised. And if Christ has not been raised, our preaching is useless and so is your faith.

1 Corinthians 15:1–5, 12–14

a) What are the most important things Christians have to believe according to Paul?
b) Why is the fulfilment of Scripture (the Old Testament) so important?
c) Explain why you think Paul says, 'And if Christ has not been raised, our preaching is useless and so is your faith'.

THE PLOT TO KILL JESUS AND ANOINTING AT BETHANY (14:1-11)

Mark begins his **passion story** by setting up the reasons why Jesus was finally betrayed and arrested. The story of the Anointing at Bethany is the moment when Judas finally makes up his mind to betray Jesus, although Mark gives us no clear reason why Judas should change his purpose from being a disciple to being a betrayer.

The whole of the passion story is written against the backdrop of the Jewish festival of **Passover**. This was one of the most ancient Jewish festivals and one which Jews throughout the world wanted to celebrate in Jerusalem. The villages around Jerusalem, such as Bethany, would have been full of pilgrims.

- The statement of the priests here is ironic and hypocritical (14:2). They say they won't arrest Jesus during the festival of the Passover, but within 24 hours they do exactly that. Mark goes on to show how they broke other Jewish rules, such as having Jesus tried for **blasphemy** at night time.
- The story contrasts various characters. Firstly, the contrast is between the devotion of the woman who spends a whole year's wages (300 denarii) on perfume and the self-righteous criticisms of the others at the meal (which presumably includes the disciples and Judas) that she should have given it to the poor (14:5).
- The woman's act of anointing is a symbol of Jesus' messiahship as king. But unlike the anointing of kings in the Old Testament, Jesus is not anointed by a priest but by an unknown woman who is prepared to sacrifice almost everything. Many modern feminist Christian writers comment that Jesus chose her and not the male disciples as an example of true discipleship when he said, 'What she has done will be told, in memory of her' (14:9).

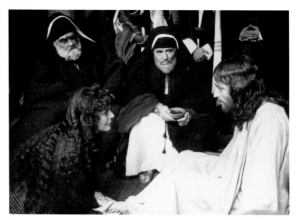

Why does a woman anoint Jesus with very expensive perfume?

> She did what she could. She poured perfume on my body beforehand to prepare for my burial. I tell you the truth, wherever the gospel is preached throughout the world, what she has done will also be told, in memory of her.
>
> *Mark 14:8–9*

So what had prompted Judas to betray Jesus?

- Maybe Mark is suggesting that Judas finally understood at Bethany that Jesus was not the kind of messiah he had been looking forward to. Jesus is depicted as a suffering servant whose Kingdom was inclusive of women and other marginalised members of society.
- Perhaps he had zealot-type hopes for a new political Kingdom much closer to the kind Jesus had indicated at the feeding of the 5000 when he organised the ordinary people in rows as if for a political revolution (Mark 6:39-40). [See page 112.]
- Maybe he thought that handing Jesus over to the authorities would force Jesus into making a political move.
- Mark only gives one reason: that Judas may have wanted money (14:11). John's Gospel records that Judas kept the communal purse (John 12:6) for the disciples' expenditures, so maybe he had just become plain greedy.

Why did Judas betray Jesus to the Jewish authorities?

LAST SUPPER (14:17–31)

KEY QUESTION

Why did Jesus choose to use the symbols of blood and bread to remember his life?
What is the significance of Jesus' Last Supper for Christians?

St Paul rarely referred explicitly to events within Jesus' life in his letters, so when in one of his letters (1 Corinthians 11:23–26) he outlines Jesus' last supper we know that for the early Christians this was an extremely important moment. Paul links the meal with Jesus' arrest on the evening of the Passover meal.

As a Passover seder meal, the unleavened bread that Jesus shares with his disciples symbolises the bread of affliction and suffering that the Jews had eaten as they escaped from Egypt. The various herbs into which the bread was dipped (Mark 14:20) not only indicated the good and harsh times experienced in Egypt, but throughout Jewish history ever since. Traditionally, there would also have been four cups of wine drunk to represent the four promises God made to the Jews as a reminder of his covenant with them as his chosen people.

TASK BOX

a) Give three reasons why Judas may have wanted to betray Jesus.
b) Debate or discuss the following in class:
* 'Judas was evil.'
* 'Judas was misled by the Jewish authorities.'
* 'Judas was politically ambitious and hoped he could provoke Jesus into acting to liberate Israel.'

Jesus eats his last Passover meal with the disciples. The big plate in the centre contains various symbolic foods as reminders of the Jews' escape from Egypt.

God's Four Promises remembered at Passover:
'I am the Lord, and I will lead you out from the under the Egyptian yoke.'
'I will deliver you from their bondage.'
'I will redeem you with an outstretched arm with great acts of judgement.'
'I will take you as My people, and I will be your God.'

So, it wasn't difficult for Jesus to give added significance to all these symbols.

- The bread (14:22) represents Jesus' body. By 'body' he would have meant his whole personality. This reinforces his claim that his death as a sacrifice was exactly what he intended and not a mistake or an unfortunate error of judgement. He is laying down his life for others on their behalf.

- The cup of wine now represents Jesus' blood of the covenant (14:23). What does this mean? In the Old Testament Moses used animals' blood, which he sprinkled over the ark of the covenant and over the people (Exodus 24:3–8). This strange ritual was to symbolise the life-giving power of blood to bind the people to God's covenant. But blood was also associated with the Passover lamb's blood that was painted over the doors of Jewish homes on the night of the escape from Egypt so that the Angel of Death would not kill them. Now Jesus is suggesting that he is the sacrifice that binds the people to God in a new and personal way and brings new life 'for many' (14:24). This is a new way of understanding the Passover wine. St Paul says that this is a *new* covenant (and some very ancient manuscript versions of Mark add this important word). The prophet Jeremiah also looked forward to a new covenant that would be established through love and not animal sacrifices. Jesus may well have had this in mind as well.

TASK BOX

a) What is a covenant?
b) Explain with reference to the Old Testament how Jesus' last supper symbolised his idea of the covenant.
c) Find out about and describe **two** of the following Church practices of the Last Supper: Anglican, Roman Catholic, Methodist, Lutheran, United Reformed, Orthodox.

The bread and wine in a modern Eucharist reminds a Christian of Jesus' body and blood.

PERSPECTIVES

The meaning of the celebration of the Last Supper today

For modern Christians the celebration of the Last Supper is an important part of worship, but there are very different interpretations of its meaning. You will see that different Christian traditions give it different titles such as: the Eucharist (meaning 'to give thanks' as in Mark 14:22), Mass (from the Latin phrase in the Roman Catholic service meaning 'to be sent out' into the world to live a Christian life), Holy Communion (stressing the way in which Jesus' death brings Christians together as a community), The Lord's Supper (used by St Paul to stress the way in which Jesus' life is to be remembered) and the Breaking of Bread (used in Acts of the Apostles to emphasise the meal as a means of fellowship and sharing). Along with baptism, many Christians believe the Eucharist is a sacrament that is an outward sign of God's love or grace. But this is interpreted in very different ways today.

Memorial. Many Protestant Christians consider the Lord's Supper to be a time to think and remember what Jesus did and that his life was a sacrifice of love for others. When they celebrate the Lord's Supper the key words are, 'Do this in remembrance of me' (1 Corinthians 11:24–25). The ceremony therefore brings Christians together as a community and reminds them that they too should be making sacrifices for others.

Consubstantiation. The Lutheran Church teaches that when the bread and wine are blessed the spirit of the risen Jesus joins with the bread and wine so that his body and blood exist side by side. Luther illustrated this with the example of an iron that is put into a fire. The fire and iron are united to make the iron red hot, but neither the fire nor the iron is changed.

Real presence. In addition to memorial, some Christians (many Anglican and Orthodox Christians) also believe that the wine and bread are not just reminders of Jesus' death but outward and visible signs of his spiritual presence whenever the Eucharist is celebrated. They consider the words 'this is my body' and 'this is my blood' (Mark 14:22 and 24) to be more than just symbols, but a moment when Christ is really present in the bread and wine at the moment of communion.

Transubstantiation. In addition to memorial and presence, many Christians (most Roman Catholics) also believe that in some mysterious way the bread and wine actually become the body and blood of Jesus. The reasons for this are philosophically complex, but this idea is based on the idea that everything is composed of two elements, substance (what it appears to be) and essence (what it actually is). A table may be made of wood, its substance, but its essence or form (its 'tableness') cannot be seen but is just known. Therefore when the priest celebrates the Mass, what changes is not the outward appearance of bread or wine but its inner essence.

THE GARDEN OF GETHSEMANE AND ARREST (14:27–52)

After the Last Supper, Mark's retelling of Jesus' anguish at Gethsemane illustrates Jesus as the suffering servant. As a human he is physically weak and spiritually wretched. John's Gospel omits the scene, perhaps because he feels it undermines Jesus' divinity and unique relationship with God. But in Mark's story the contrast is between Jesus and his disciples. Whereas Jesus overcomes the temptation to give up and ask God to 'take this cup from me' (14:36), the disciples fall asleep (14:37), exhausted and physically weak. But ironically when he says to them, 'The spirit is willing, but the body is weak' (14:38) it quickly turns out that even this is untrue, for later when Jesus is arrested the disciples all run away (14:50).

 Abba, Father, everything is possible for you. Take this cup from me. Yet not what I will, but what you will.

Mark 14:36

Jesus' prayer to God, however, shows just how close this situation places him in his relationship with God. He uses the term *abba*, the affectionate term for father or daddy (14:36).

The cup is the cup of suffering. Earlier, Jesus had told James and John that they would drink this cup (10:39) as a sign of their deaths as martyrs, so it indicates here that Jesus knows of his own imminent martyrdom and the fulfilment of his three passion predictions about his fate as the Son of Man.

 The three passion predictions are Mark 8:31, 9:30–32 and 10:32–34.

He said to them, 'The Son of Man is going to be betrayed into the hands of men. They will kill him, and after three days he will rise.'

Mark 9:31

The role of Judas contrasts with the failure of the disciples. Whereas they fail due to human weakness, Judas' action is deliberate. Mark calls him the betrayer (14:44) and his action of kissing Jesus as the usual act of trust and affection between rabbi (teacher) and pupil underlines just how despicable he is. Judas' kiss also illustrates that in Jerusalem few know who Jesus is, for the crowd (14:43), sent by the **Sanhedrin**, come unnecessarily armed with weapons to arrest what they imagine must be a dangerous rebel.

TEST YOURSELF

1 Why will the woman's act at Bethany be remembered throughout the world?
2 Give two reasons why Judas may have betrayed Jesus.
3 What does Jesus say the bread and wine now symbolise at the Last Supper?
4 Give two names Christians use today when they remember the Last Supper.
5 What do the disciples do whilst Jesus prays at Gethsemane?
6 In his prayer at Gethsemane what does Jesus ask God to do?

THE JEWISH AND ROMAN TRIALS
(14:53–15:15)

KEY QUESTION

Why was Jesus tried by both the Jewish and Roman authorities?

Jesus is tried twice, first by the Jewish senior authorities, or the Sanhedrin, and secondly by Pontius Pilate, the Roman governor of Palestine at that time. Why is this? The arrest of Jesus is because he is not only a troublemaker but, more importantly, he has been attacking the Jewish authorities and claiming to have a higher authority than they have. In Jewish law this is blasphemy which carries with it capital punishment (Leviticus 24:10–16). However, according to Roman law, the Jewish authorities were not allowed to put a person to death on capital charges as this could only happen if the culprit had committed a capital offence according to Roman law. So the second trial is to establish whether Jesus, the troublemaker, is indeed a threat to Roman rule. To find him guilty of **treason** would give Pilate a good reason to put Jesus to death. But both trials show just how difficult it was to establish that Jesus had committed either blasphemy or treason.

The High Priest in ceremonial clothes.

The trial in front of the High Priest
(14:53–15:1)

The High Priest is the judge. He is not named in Mark, but Matthew rightly identifies him as Caiaphas (Matthew 26:57). Technically, the trial is illegal and certainly confused. According to Jewish law:

- A trial for capital punishment, that is one which carried the death penalty, could not take place at night, and Mark makes it clear that it is late at night (14:17).
- The trial had to have reliable witnesses, and Mark relates how the witnesses did not agree (14:57) and confused Jesus' words about destroying the Temple (14:68) – when he had in fact predicted that the Temple would be destroyed at the coming of the Kingdom (13:1–2).

 Pilate said to them, 'Take him yourselves and judge him by your own law.' The Jews said to him, 'It is not lawful for us to put any man to death.'

John 18:31

In capital cases they hold trial during the daytime and the verdict must also be reached during the daytime.

Mishnah Sanhedrin 4:1

John's Gospel and the Jewish law (in the Mishnah) both support the view that Jesus' trial was illegal. But there is considerable dispute amongst scholars over whether the trial was a proper trial and what its purpose was.

It is therefore rather surprising that the High Priest asks Jesus to defend himself because so far there is nothing to defend himself against. Mark records that Jesus 'was silent and made no answer' (14:61). Why did Jesus not answer? Perhaps he felt that whatever he said would be misunderstood. Maybe he now felt himself to be in exactly the same position as the Suffering

Servant described by Isaiah. When the innocent Servant is attacked by all around him, Isaiah says 'He was oppressed, and he was afflicted, yet he opened not his mouth; like a lamb that is led to the slaughter, and like a sheep before its shearers is dumb, so he opened not his mouth' (Isaiah 53:7). There is good reason to suppose that Mark wished to depict Jesus as the Suffering Servant, because in Isaiah's account the servant's death, as a result of human maliciousness, is presented as a sacrifice for their sinful behaviour and the means by which his accusers are forgiven.

> ## KEY QUESTION
>
> Did Jesus commit blasphemy? What is Mark's view of the Jewish authorities?

Had Jesus committed blasphemy? Mark's account is far from clear. It is possible that his attacks on keeping the Sabbath (2:23–28 and 3:1–6) or his cleansing of the Temple (11:15–18) were considered blasphemous, but none of his criticisms of Judaism were sufficient to have him put to death. The only option left to the High Priest is to ask Jesus himself where he thinks he gets his authority from.

- The High Priest asks, 'Are you the Christ, the Son of the Blessed One?' (14:61). In other words he is asking very explicitly whether Jesus thinks he is the messiah sent by God. If Jesus does think this, then the meeting would have to establish whether Jesus' claim was genuine or not. To claim to be a messiah was not in itself blasphemous.
- Jesus replies, 'I am; and you will see the Son of Man sitting at the right hand of the Mighty One, and coming on the clouds of heaven.' (14:62). Unlike the time when he discussed his identity with the disciples at Caesarea Philippi (8:30–31), Jesus now makes it very clear that he is the messiah. But in the second part of his statement he tells the High Priest that as God's messiah it is he who will judge him, not the other way round. It is not clear exactly when Jesus thinks this will be. It could

be after his resurrection or when he returns to bring in the Kingdom of God as he described in the Little Apocalypse (13:26). Jesus' return is known as the 'parousia'. This is probably why he uses the term Son of Man, because in the Old Testament the role of the Son of Man, in the book of Daniel (7:13), is to assist God or 'the Mighty One' to judge the world and gather the good people into the Kingdom.

- 'And the high priest tore his garments and said, "Why do we still need witnesses? You have heard his blasphemy"' (14:63). According to Jewish custom the High Priest would tear his robe as a sign that the accused had spoken a blasphemy and the trial therefore had ended. But has Jesus really committed a blasphemy? He has not actually said the word 'God' but the indirect term 'the Mighty One'. Perhaps the High Priest objects when Jesus says 'I am' (14:62), for God's name revealed to Moses is 'I am' (Exodus 3:14) and can never be said. Whatever the case, the High Priest considers Jesus to be guilty, the Sanhedrin agrees and condemns him to death. According to Jewish law this would normally have been done by stoning (Leviticus 24:10–16), but, as we have seen, in this case the penalty could only be carried out by the Romans.

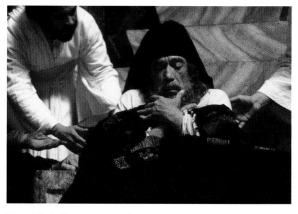

The High Priest tore his clothes as a sign that the accused had committed blasphemy.

- The mocking that follows (14:65) is a reminder again that Jesus is the Suffering Servant, and Mark echoes the details of Isaiah (50:6) when he says that the attendants at the trial spit at and slap his face. They don't mock him as a messiah but as a false prophet, because the false prophet claimed to be bringing God's word and would therefore be leading the people astray. The charge for false prophecy is death (Deuteronomy 18:20) – but none of this has been debated in the trial. It is another example of the whole muddle of the occasion.

- Peter's denial (14:66–72) of Jesus three times over, contrasts with Jesus' silence against the false accusations. Peter is rightly asked whether he is from Galilee (his accent probably gave him away) and whether he is a follower of Jesus. But Peter fails this 'mini-trial'. Peter's weakness is one of Mark's themes; even the closest disciples found it extremely difficult to be true followers of Jesus. Peter weeps (14:72) because he knows he has done wrong. He is forgiven specifically at the resurrection (16:7) when the angel says that Jesus will meet Peter and the other disciples in Galilee.

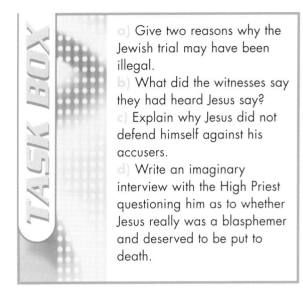

TASK BOX

a) Give two reasons why the Jewish trial may have been illegal.

b) What did the witnesses say they had heard Jesus say?

c) Explain why Jesus did not defend himself against his accusers.

d) Write an imaginary interview with the High Priest questioning him as to whether Jesus really was a blasphemer and deserved to be put to death.

The trial in front of Pilate (15:2–15)

KEY QUESTION

What kind of person is Pilate?

After a brief meeting very early in the morning the Sanhedrin probably agreed they would say to Pilate (15:1) that Jesus has set himself up as king to rival the authority of Rome. As 'messiah' or 'christ' could also mean 'king', the Sanhedrin only had to shift their evidence to indicate that Jesus was not just religiously dangerous but also a political threat to the stability of the nation.

- Jesus' reply of 'Yes, it is as you say' (15:2) to Pilate's charge that he is the 'King of the Jews' is designed to make Pilate entirely responsible for the outcome, because Jesus is 'king' in the sense of being the messiah, but not a king as a military leader.

- The crowd wanted Barabbas released, a man who really has committed murder and has been charged with treason (15:7). He might have belonged to one of the extreme Zealot groups. So, the story emphasises the increasing injustice of the situation. A guilty man is released and an innocent man is condemned to death as a troublemaker.

Again the high priest asked him, 'Are you the Christ, the Son of the Blessed One?' 'I am,' said Jesus. 'And you will see the Son of Man sitting at the right hand of the Mighty One and coming on the cloud of heaven.' The High Priest tore his clothes. 'Why do we need any more witnesses?' he asked. 'You have heard the blasphemy. What do you think?' They all condemned him as worthy of death.

Mark 14:61–64

The blasphemer is not culpable unless he pronounces the Name itself.

Mishnah Sanhedrin 7:5

Did Jesus actually say the Name (of God) and commit blasphemy according to the Jewish law stated in the Mishnah?

Mark presents Pilate as a person looking to keep the crowds quiet (15:8), even though he knows that they have been stirred up by the chief priests and that their accusations are false and made out of jealousy for Jesus' following. But is it likely that Pilate would have been so weak-willed he would have been persuaded by the crowds to kill an innocent man and allowed a murderer to go free. As he says, 'Why, what evil has he done?' (15:14). Perhaps he felt that with the enormous crowds present in Jerusalem that day, the death of one man to solve a potentially dangerous situation would be better than having a riot on his hands if he failed to act.

So Pilate is persuaded by the crowds and has Jesus flogged (15:15). Flogging was often used for troublemakers and was the first of the tor-ments before crucifixion. The leather straps used to flog the condemned man also had small metal spikes attached so that they tore at the flesh.

 Philo describes Pilate in his *De Legatione ad Gaium 28* as an 'inflexible, merciless and obstinate' man.

So would Pilate really have given in to the crowd or the chief priests so easily?

 **TASK BOX**

a) Explain why Pilate accuses Jesus of being 'King of the Jews'.
b) Give three examples of the way in which Pilate shows that he thinks Jesus is innocent.
c) **Either**: Discuss whether Mark thinks that Pilate was responsible for Jesus' death. **Or**: Conduct your own imaginary trial of Pilate after Jesus' death to decide on Pilate's motives and guilt/innocence. Your witnesses could include senior Jewish authorities, some of Jesus' disciples, and an acquaintance of Pilate (as a character witness).

Jesus is flogged before being crucified according to Roman custom.

TEST YOURSELF

1 What do the witnesses accuse Jesus of having said or done at the High Priest's trial?
2 What question does the High Priest ask Jesus?
3 Why does the High Priest rip his clothes?
4 Outline what happened when Peter denied knowing Jesus.
5 What had Barabbas done?
6 On what charge does Pilate con-demn Jesus to death?
7 What does Jesus say to Pilates' charge?

JESUS' DEATH (15:16–47)

KEY QUESTION

Did Jesus have to die?

Crucifixion was the Roman method of putting slaves, violent criminals and rebels against Rome to death. It was a terrible form of punishment, designed to be slow and very public so as to be as much a deterrent as possible. Nails were often banged through the wrists and anklebones of the condemned man onto a wooden cross. Death was not caused by blood loss but through exhaustion and, because the lungs slowly filled up with mucus, asphyxiation.

But for Mark the importance of Jesus' death is the theological details that depict him as the Suffering Servant dying for the sins of others. Having seen Jesus in his divine role as the messiah who will help God judge the world, in this scene he is the human being undergoing extreme pain and suffering.

The key features of Jesus' crucifixion are as follows:

- The Roman soldier makes a crown of thorns (15:16–20) to mock Jesus as the 'King of the Jews' (15:32). Although they think he is a false king, for Mark he actually *is* a king but not in a political sense. The crown of thorns could be an object of torture, although it is more likely that the thorns would be facing outwards to be like the rays of the sun – just in the same way as the Roman coins at the time depicted the Roman emperors. The soldiers dress Jesus in purple, also the colour of the emperor, and pretend to pay homage to him as a king. Jesus is further mocked by the passers-by and even by those who are crucified with him.

The crucifixion. The titulus above Jesus' head said that he was 'King of the Jews'.

 Jesus' final words from Psalm 22

My God, my God, why have you forsaken me?
Why are you so far from saving me, so far from the words of my groaning? ...
Yet you are enthroned as the Holy One; you are the praise of Israel.
In you our fathers put their trust.

Psalm 22:1 and 3–4

Jesus cried out in a loud voice, '*Eloi Eloi lama sabachthani?*', which means, 'My God, my God why have you forsaken me?'

Mark 15:34

Other details from the psalm must have affected Mark's telling of Jesus' death: the sharing out of his clothes by casting lots (15:24, see Psalm 22:18), and the insults of the passers by (15:29, see Psalm 22:7).

- Is Jesus' cry from the cross, 'My God, my God, why have you forsaken me?' (15:34), one of hope or despair? His words quote the opening of Psalm 22, the evening prayer said by pious Jews. Perhaps Jesus' cry is simply as a mortal man dying in the anguish of death and despair that God has not saved him. Or Jesus' cry could be as a holy man saying his prayer of hope and obedience to God – the way in which Psalm 22 continues. In Luke's Gospel, Jesus' cry is altered to, 'Into your hands I commit my spirit' (Luke 23:46) – maybe that is what Jesus means. Luke certainly appears to have toned down the sense of failure that in Mark's Gospel Jesus seems to express. Mark also records that Jesus said the prayer in Aramaic (a type of Hebrew), probably because the first word 'My God' or 'Eloi' is misheard by the passers-by as a cry to Elijah. They tease him about being the failed martyr who thinks that Elijah (the great Old Testament prophet who many believed had not died but was taken into heaven) will come and rescue him from the cross in his time of trouble.

Jesus cries from the cross. Was his cry one of despair or hope?

- The splitting of the Temple curtain (15:38) is a powerful symbol of the new relationship that Jesus' death has now established between God and people. The curtain separated the Holy place from the Holy of Holies (Exodus 40:2) and could only be passed once a year on the Day of Atonement when the High Priest acted as mediator between people and God. Jesus' death removes the barrier. Now everybody may offer their sins directly to God and seek his forgiveness. The Temple and all its sacrifices are replaced by Jesus' sacrifice on the cross. Although Mark's teaching is not clearly spelt out, this is the nearest he gets to illustrating that Jesus, the Son of Man, dies as a 'ransom for many' (10:45). His readers would have understood that a ransom would have to be paid to set a slave free, as when God freed the Israelites from slavery in Egypt (Isaiah 43:3). Now Jesus' death frees humans from what St Paul called the 'slavery of sin'.

- The centurion's remark (15:39) is ambiguous. Some translations say, 'Surely this man was *a* son of God', a hero in the Roman religion. Other translations read 'Surely this man was *the* Son of God', in which case it is not Jesus' miracles or even his teaching that reveal his identity but the manner and example of his death. Mark may have liked the fact that it was a non-Jew who was able to realise the truth and was the first to be affected by the symbolic action of the Temple's curtain. Of course the centurion may not have meant that Jesus was God, but in the second translation he would have meant that the nature of Jesus' death was unique in his willingness to die for his God. Even Peter, his closest friend, has not understood this yet.

- The central Christian teaching that St Paul passed on to his Christian communities (look back to page 79 of this Unit) made quite an explicit reference to Jesus' burial (15:40–47). This is because, even from very early times, rumours had developed that either Jesus had not died or that his body had been stolen by his followers who then claimed that he had been resurrected. That is why the gospels, as well as the earliest summaries of Christian belief, stressed the fact that Jesus had been buried.

- Why are the women (15:40–41) alone here at the tomb and not the disciples? The presence of the women at the cross contrasts with the disciples' absence and therefore lack of faith. Despite his earlier protestations that he would stay with Jesus to the end, even Peter fled. It is these women disciples, who have remained with Jesus all the way from Galilee, (15:41) who see Jesus' death and are the first witnesses of the resurrection. Both occasions are indications of the radical nature of the Kingdom of God which accepts *all* people regardless of gender and social standing and reverses the role of women from mere bystanders in Judaism to active and liberated members of the new life (the Kingdom of God). They must be important because Mark lists them by name: Mary Magdalene, Mary (the mother of James the younger and Joses), and Salome. They see where Jesus is laid so they know where to come to give the body its full burial rites on the first day of the week.

- Joseph of Arimathea's significance (15:43) is primarily because he is a member of the Sanhedrin. It indicates that at Jesus' trial not all members (around 71) had joined the High Priest and the members of the Sanhedrin in the charge of blasphemy against Jesus – even though Mark says they all condemned Jesus (14:64). Many intelligent and influential Jews realised that Jesus' teaching on the Kingdom was not a threat to Judaism. As a sign of Joseph's devotion, he provides a place in the family tomb for Jesus' body. As a rich man the entrance to Joseph of Arimathea's tomb would have been covered by a large rolling stone a bit like a mill wheel. As it is now

evening (15:42) it means that it is now the start of the Sabbath and so Joseph has to bend several Sabbath rules to bury Jesus quickly according to Jewish custom, one of which is to buy a linen sheet (15:46) to wrap up the corpse.

A first-century tomb and rolling stone.

TEST YOURSELF

1 How do the Roman soldiers mock Jesus?

2 What are Jesus' last words on the cross?

3 Why do some passers-by think Jesus was calling for Elijah?

4 Where was the curtain in the Temple that split in two?

5 What did the centurion at the cross say when he saw how Jesus died?

6 Which of Jesus' disciples remained at his cross as he died?

7 What role did Joseph of Arimathea play in Jesus' death?

> ## KEY QUESTION
> What actually happened at Jesus' resurrection?

According to the most ancient and most reliable manuscripts of Mark's Gospel, the gospel ends at 16:8 with the women running away from the tomb greatly afraid. If this is so, Mark does not really have a resurrection story as such because Jesus does not actually appear to the disciples as he does in the other gospels.

The empty tomb.

 The angel's important words to the women at the tomb:

'Don't be alarmed, you are looking for Jesus the Nazarene, who was crucified. He has risen! He is not here. See the place where they have laid him. But go and tell his disciples and Peter, "He is going ahead of you into Galilee. There you will see him, just as he told you."'

Mark 16:7

The important details of the resurrection story in 16:1–8 are:

- The story begins with the message of the young man at the tomb (16:6) who says that Jesus is not dead but will meet the disciples in Galilee. The young man is a divine messenger or angel (suggested by his white robe) and therefore his primary purpose is to convey the hope of the resurrection experience as a message. Because Mark does not write about a physical meeting of the risen Jesus with the women or the disciples, everything is left to the power of the message conveyed. For Mark's readers, just as much as for Christians today, belief in the resurrection depends on hearing and believing the message and not on seeing the risen Jesus, so it is possible that Mark is trying to get his readers to understand this.

- The angel's words are primarily to instruct the women to inform the disciples that Jesus has been raised (the tomb is empty) and that he will meet them and Peter in Galilee.

- The final words of the gospel refer to the women's reaction to the young man's message, 'because they were afraid' (16:8). The women's experience is not only 'fear' in its ordinary sense. The Greek word for 'fear' means religious awe and deep insight. Perhaps only now they have come to understand the real meaning of the resurrection, that it is not in a resuscitated body, but rather the spiritual reality of Jesus as a person who lives on. However, even though they might have realised this, they behave just like the male disciples before them and fail to do as they have been instructed because they 'said nothing to anyone'.

Mark's 'short ending'

But does Mark really end his gospel on such a cliffhanger? Some ancient manuscripts have what scholars call an additional short ending and others the long ending (16:9–20). The short ending is to explain that despite their silence in verse 8, the women *did* carry out their instruction from the angel and the gospel message was preached throughout the world. However, the language is unlike the rest of Mark's Gospel and many doubt that it is the original ending.

 Mark's 'short ending':

But they reported briefly to Peter and those with him all that they had been told. After this, Jesus himself sent out by means of them, from east to west, the sacred and imperishable proclamation of eternal salvation.

Mark's 'long ending'

In the long ending, Jesus appears to Mary Magdalene and she reports what she has seen to the 11 disciples who disbelieve her. Then Jesus appears to two others, but still the disciples do not believe and then, finally, he appears to the 11 whilst they are having supper and tells them off for not believing. He gives them the instruction, or commission, to preach to the whole world and to convince those they are preaching to that the disciples will be able to perform miracles (16:17), exorcise demons, speak in tongues or different languages (inspired by the Holy Spirit), pick up serpents and drink poison and not die, and heal the sick (16:18). Finally, Jesus ascends into heaven (16:19–20) and the disciples preach the good news to the whole world.

Although some argue that Mark added the long ending himself, many others feel that it has been put together using ideas from the other gospels and Acts of the Apostles. But its major problem is that it fails to follow on from 16:8. Jesus now appears to Mary Magdalene, whereas the women have just encountered the angel and run away dumbstruck. Most importantly, Jesus does not meet them in Galilee.

So, from a very long time ago the ending of Mark has been considered unsatisfactory. What remains a puzzle is why Mark stops so abruptly at verse 8, with an unfinished sentence. In Greek the last word of verse 8 is 'because', which in a literal translation means the gospel ends, 'they were afraid because'. Many have suggested that there must have been a lost ending:

- Mark would have concluded his 'good news' with a proper account of the resurrection and the 'seeing' Jesus in Galilee as 16:7 promises.
- Mark may have been interrupted, arrested maybe (perhaps during the time of Nero's persecutions), and didn't have time to finish his sentence (read pages 2–4 to remind yourself of when Mark was writing).
- The scroll may have been mutilated, perhaps due to fire, or carelessness and so the ending was lost.
- The ending may have been considered blasphemous and deliberately removed.

But all these possibilities are too trivial for such an important document. If the document was mutilated, someone would have known the ending and rewritten it from memory. It is also very unlikely that Mark would have been arrested or have died in mid-sentence without the sentence being completed by a pupil.

The alternative is that Mark intended to end at 16:8. There is no reason why, in Greek, he should not end on the word 'because'; perhaps he wanted his readers to think for themselves what the resurrection really means. After all he had already given a foretaste of Jesus' glorified state in the transfiguration (9:2–8) and, as in his argument about resurrection with the Sadducees (12:18–28), he showed them that the resurrection body is not the same as the earthly body. Therefore Mark has avoided the problem of what kind of existence Jesus would have had after he died.

Was Mark interrupted?

Was there an accident?

Could a scribe have been careless?

Is there a lost ending to Mark's Gospel?

Was the gospel considered blasphemous?

Some modern interpreters think that Mark is very cleverly suggesting that there is no ending of the gospel because the clue is given by the angel that they should 'go to Galilee' where they will see Jesus as he told them he would. But Jesus has made no earlier prediction about meeting them in Galilee. Some scholars think that Mark wanted his readers to think back to when we first saw Jesus in Galilee. When we look up this reference it is when Jesus was preaching the good news about the Kingdom of God (1:14–15) and calling his disciples to be 'fishers of men' (1:17).

So it seems that the command to go to Galilee is really about becoming a Christian and 'seeing' Jesus (16:7) in everyday life. The whole gospel provides numerous examples of how this should be done.

But many think that this interpretation is too subtle and complicated and not what Mark intended. Most of all it doesn't adequately explain what Mark believed about the actual resurrection of Jesus.

1 Outline the message of the young man at Jesus' tomb.
2 How did the women react to the young man's message?
3 What is the content of the short ending of Mark?
4 Outline the longer ending of Mark.
5 Give two reasons why there might there be a 'lost ending' of Mark.

PERSPECTIVES

What really happened at the resurrection?

There are many views as to what actually happened at Jesus' resurrection. Some doubt it altogether, others argue that it didn't happen as an actual historical event but was either just a powerful experience or symbol of Jesus' presence in their lives.

- Traditional Christians argue that Jesus was physically resurrected. The longer ending of Mark records that Jesus was able to talk to his disciples (16:14), and in the other gospels some are even able to touch him (John 20:24–29) and to see the wounds of his crucifixion (Luke 24:39).

- Others argue that Jesus was not present in actual physical terms, but appeared to his followers as a series of powerful visions. The disciples' vision of heavenly Jesus at the transfiguration (Mark 9:2–8) may be Mark's way of giving an insight as to what Jesus' resurrection will be like. There are many modern accounts where a dead person has appeared and even spoken to someone shortly after their death. Quite often these moments have occurred at times of extreme stress or anguish. For those who have experienced these moments, the vision has been very real.

- Some consider that Jesus was physically resurrected but his body wasn't an ordinary earthly kind but a transformed spiritual body. We cannot know exactly what this is, but as Jesus says to the Sadducees (Mark 12:25), in heaven the resurrected body is like an angel's. St Paul uses the term 'spiritual body' when he is describing the resurrection (1 Corinthians 15:35–46) and the longer ending of Mark describes Jesus appearing 'in another form' (Mark 16:12).

- More radical opinion is sceptical about whether we can know anything about the historical reliability of the resurrection accounts. For example, the evidence in the New Testament about Jesus' resurrection appearances are contradictory. Some suggest that he continued to appear to people for many years – St Paul reports having such a vision at least ten years later (1 Corinthians 15:8). Other accounts say that his appearances lasted only for a few months before he ascended into heaven (Mark 16:19 and Acts 1:9). Many radicals doubt whether the tomb was really empty and argue that the 'empty tomb' idea was invented to explain the symbolism of the resurrection. They also argue that as the list of women at the tomb varies – they are not mentioned by Paul at all (1 Corinthians 15:5–6) – the early writers probably added them as witnesses to the resurrection as the male disciples had fled earlier at Gethsemane (Mark 14:50). Radicals argue that the real resurrection was the spiritual experience and presence of Jesus in the hearts of his followers and the hope that he gave them.

- Those who doubt the resurrection altogether argue that Jesus' body might have been stolen and that his followers invented a story to cover up the loss of their hero. This was a very ancient objection and Matthew records it in his gospel (Matthew 28:11–15). Others argue that Jesus' resurrection appearances were the result of mass hysteria or wish fulfilment caused by extreme grief.

Was Jesus physically raised from the dead or was his resurrection a symbol of hope invented by his followers?

WHY DID JESUS HAVE TO DIE?

How can the death of a man 2000 years ago have any effect on humans today? The question is no different for us than for those who first pondered on the meaning of Jesus' death in the very early days. One answer is given in John's Gospel, that Jesus is 'the Lamb of God who takes away the sin of the world' (John 1:29). But how can the death of one man take away sin? For centuries Christians have struggled to explain what this means, even if the basic idea of Christian salvation is a sense of being freed and able to start again. This is sometimes called atonement, which means to make amends, to heal and establish a new relationship.

Mark describes Jesus' death as a sacrifice and atonement. He quotes the metaphor Jesus uses which describes his death as a ransom (10:45). Mark lived during Roman rule, so the hope that all slaves could buy their freedom would have been an amazing and impossible thought. A ransom for many therefore means that someone had bought the freedom for all those who were enslaved to others.

> For even the Son of Man did not come to be served, but to serve, and to give his life as a ransom for many.

Mark 10:45

This is my blood of the covenant which is poured out for many.

Mark 14:24

Both these key passages suggest how Jesus is the means of salvation for Christians according to Mark's Gospel.

Christians have often tried to explain how Jesus' sacrifice works as an atonement. Here are three views:

- In the victory view, sin is very real and dangerous because after Adam and Eve have sinned so much, all humans are held as slaves by Satan. Only the person who is without sin and can resist its temptations is able to free humans by offering himself on the behalf of humans. That person is Jesus. If his death appears to be a victory of Satan, this is reversed by the resurrection which is the triumph of good over evil.

- In the satisfaction view, the question asked is why has God allowed humans to suffer so long in their guilt? The explanation is that God has wanted 'satisfaction' or a sign that humans are truly sorry for their rejection of his love. It becomes clear that no human is good enough ever to manage this. But as God is also a God of love he sends his only Son on the behalf of humans to pay off their guilt by making the ultimate sacrifice for them through his death and so satisfy both his anger and sadness. The resurrection is a sign that Jesus has not died in vain and that life after death is a reward to all those who follow in his example and teaching.

- The moral view puts the emphasis on the human response to God's love, which he demonstrated in the death and selfless giving of Jesus on the cross. Salvation is achieved because humans are so emotionally moved by their own sense of guilt that they repent and ask for God's forgiveness. If there are debts to be paid, then the Christian pays them in his or her daily life by living morally with others. Resurrection is a symbol of the new life after repentance.

Jesus' death is often seen as a victory over evil – or Satan.

For many Christians Jesus' death is a gift to God, which pays off their sins.

Many Christians think Jesus' death is an example of love, which makes them want to repent and pray for forgiveness.

A New Approach – St Mark's Gospel

Oscar Romero

A martyr is a Christian who dies because of their faith in God. Their deaths follow the example of Jesus – that to be committed to Christianity may sometimes require the ultimate sacrifice of death. But just as Jesus' death established a new relationship between God and humans, the death of the martyr also helps Christians create a better world. A good example is that of Oscar Romero, archbishop of El Salvador in Latin America. He became increasingly aware that the Church had failed to support the millions of poor people in his country to resist exploitation by the rich and the powerful. Romero knew that to side with the poor, just as Jesus had sided with the outcasts, the poor and the weak, would make him a dangerous rebel in the eyes of the government. Romero preached that it was every soldier's Christian duty to resist carrying out government orders that resulted in the oppression of the poor and the killing of all those who helped them. Shortly before his assassination, Romero said,

A Salvadorean views a picture of Oscar Romero.

'Christ invites us not to fear persecution. Believe me, brothers and sisters, anyone committed to the poor must suffer the same fate as the poor. And in El Salvador we know the fate of the poor; to be taken away, to be tortured, to be jailed, to be found dead'.

On 23 March 1980, whilst celebrating Mass, Oscar Romero was shot dead. But his death inspired almost 100,000 Christians and non-Christian revolutionaries to come together in solidarity and to express their will in resisting the exploitation of the poor and need for a democratic government. As one priest said of him:

'With Archbishop Romero, God has visited El Salvador'.

Romero's death is an inspiration to many. From a Christian perspective, his death was a victory over political corruption and a triumph for the weak and oppressed. His most famous saying has become:

'I must tell you, as a Christian, I do not believe in death without resurrection. If I am killed, I shall arise in the Salvadorean people'.

Did Romero's death achieve more than his life as a priest and bishop?

TASK BOX

a) What does salvation mean?

b) Explain the religious reasons why Jesus was condemned to death by the Sanhedrin.

c) Explain the political reasons why Jesus was condemned to death by Pontius Pilate.

d) Explain three ways in which Christians have explained Jesus' death as a sacrifice for their sins.

e) In two columns set out the arguments for and against the possibility of resurrection and life after death.

---

1 a. What is crucifixion? [2]

b. Describe the trial of Jesus before the High Priest. [6]

c. Explain why the events of the Last Supper are important for Christians. [8]

d. 'Jesus' death is more important than his resurrection.'
Do you agree? Give reasons for your opinion, showing you have considered another point of view. In your answer you should refer to Mark's Gospel. [4]

2 a. Describe what happened at the Last Supper, according to Mark's Gospel. [8]

b. Explain how the Last Supper influences Christian worship today. [7]

c. 'The main point of the Eucharist is remembering something that happened a long time ago.'
Do you agree? Give reasons to support your answer and show that you have thought about different points of view. [5]

Assignment

WEBLINKS

- Arguments about the resurrection of Jesus: www.riverpower.org/resurrection.htm
- On the meaning and celebration of the Eucharist: www.wcc-coe.org/wcc/what/faith/bem4.html
- On a Protestant meaning and celebration of the Lord's Supper: www.oldfirstchurch.org/lords-supper.html
- How Judas has been portrayed in film: www.hamilton.edu/academic/Religious/mijangos.html

REMEMBER

▶ Jesus was condemned to death for blasphemy by the Jewish authorities.

▶ Jesus was condemned to death for treason by Pontius Pilate for the Roman authorities.

▶ Without the resurrection Jesus would have died merely as a teacher and prophet.

▶ Mark wishes to show how Jesus truly suffered as a human being and yet was divine as God's Son.

UNIT EIGHT | Who is Jesus?

8

KEY WORDS

Christ/messiah: The two terms from the Greek and Hebrew words meaning 'anointed one'. They quickly came to describe Jesus' special relationship with God. Originally, messiah referred to a military figure such as King David.

Messianic secret: The term used by scholars to refer to the several occasions when Jesus commanded people or evil spirits to be silent about his identity.

Saviour: 'One who saves' or 'heals'. The title is not used in Mark but it is implied by all Jesus' miracles when he heals, forgives, provides and rescues.

Son of God: In the Old Testament this referred either to the king or to Israel or to a righteous person. The gospels use it to refer to Jesus' special relationship with God. The title is never used by Jesus.

Son of Man: Is only used by Jesus to describe his role as 'man for others', a suffering servant and God's chosen one who would judge on earth and in heaven.

WHO DO PEOPLE SAY JESUS IS?

The New Testament depicts Jesus in many different ways, as can been seen from the wide range of titles that are used to describe him: the 'Rock', the 'Lamb of God', the 'Pioneer', the 'Good Shepherd', the 'Word', the 'High Priest' and so on. Artists over the centuries have continued to present Jesus in ways that attempt to express how, as a human being, Jesus experiences all that humans do. Some pictures show Jesus as a woman or as a black person.

But for all the writers of the New Testament Jesus was more than just a man, he was in some special way also God's Son and one who had a unique and special relationship with God. Some writers simply said that he was God. None of the New Testament writers attempt to explain exactly how Jesus could be human and divine, but it has been a major debating point in theology for centuries.

- For liberal Christians today, Jesus is a human being who had an extraordinary insight and relationship with God and was able to express this in his life and teaching. He had what is sometimes called perfect God-consciousness. Liberals consider Jesus' miracles and resurrection to be powerful symbols of his unique personality and the hope that he gave and gives to others.

- For traditional Christians, Jesus is 'fully man and fully God'. This is the phrase the Church agreed on at a meeting in 451 CE at Chalcedon and has become part of the creeds that Christians recite as part of their regular prayers. For traditionalists (fundamentalists and conservatives), Jesus' miracles are especially important in establishing his divinity as God, because unlike other prophets who were able to perform miracles because God was working through them, Jesus performed his own miracles because he was God.

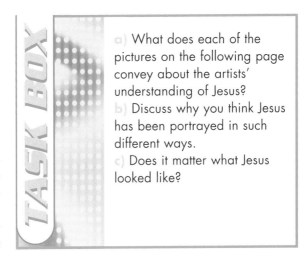

TASK BOX

a) What does each of the pictures on the following page convey about the artists' understanding of Jesus?
b) Discuss why you think Jesus has been portrayed in such different ways.
c) Does it matter what Jesus looked like?

Why has Jesus been portrayed in so many ways?

A New Approach – St Mark's Gospel

Jesus left there and went to his home town, accompanied by his disciples. When the Sabbath came, he began to teach in the synagogue, and many who heard him were amazed. 'Where did this man get these things?' they asked. 'What's this wisdom that has been given him, that he even does miracles! Isn't this the carpenter? Isn't this Mary's son and the brother of James, Joseph, Judas and Simon? Aren't his sisters here with us?' And they took offence at him. Jesus said to them, 'Only in his home town, among his relatives and in his own house is a prophet without honour.' He could not do any miracles there, except lay his hands on a few sick people and heal them. And he was amazed at their lack of faith.

Mark 6:1–6

a) Imagine you are one of the members of the congregation at the synagogue where Jesus has been teaching. Write your own diary entry and express your thoughts.
b) Why do members of his own town take 'offence' in Jesus' teaching?
c) Why is Jesus unable to perform any miracles?
d) Write down three reasons why you think Mark has included this story, which doubts Jesus' role as messiah.
e) Read Luke 1:26–38. Do you think Mark knows the story? Give reasons for your answer.

Jesus: man and God

The beginning of the gospel about Jesus Christ the Son of God.

Mark 1:1

The Word became flesh and made his dwelling amongst us.

John 1:14

Jesus of Nazareth was a man accredited by God to you by miracles, wonders and signs, which God did among you through him.

Acts 2:22

Perfect God, and Perfect Man: of a reasonable soul and human flesh subsisting; equal to the Father, as touching his Godhead; and inferior to the Father, as touching his Manhood, who although he be God and Man; yet he is not two, but one Christ.

Athanasian Creed

Jesus is given various titles in Mark's Gospel: Son of God, Son of Man, the messiah, the Son of David and Saviour. Each one attempts to explain an aspect of Jesus' identity and purpose.

JESUS: HUMAN AND DIVINE

KEY QUESTION

Did Mark know that Jesus had a miraculous birth?

There is no single idea in the Old Testament that is associated with the messiah. **Messiah** (or 'Christ' in Greek) simply means the 'anointed one', that is, a person specially chosen by God to establish his law and judge the people. By the first century he was sometimes described as a divine being, like an angel, who would assist God in establishing the age to come or God's perfect Kingdom on earth. But in Judaism there is never any suggestion that the messiah would be more than an angel, certainly never divine as God. Such an idea would have been blasphemous in first-century Jewish thought.

But Mark is quite clear from his very first verse that Jesus is the messiah, both human and divine, although he is unclear exactly how this is so. Does he believe, like the author of John's Gospel, that Jesus is God? Mark's Jesus is an enigmatic or mysterious figure whose divinity is slowly revealed through his life and finally in the promise of being 'seen' by the disciples after the resurrection. Unlike Matthew and Luke, Mark has no story of Jesus' special birth, so does it mean that Mark is unaware of what is sometimes referred to as Mary's virgin birth?

The passage from Mark 6:1–6 tells us a lot about how Mark understands Jesus.

- Mark uses the term Jesus and not Jesus Christ as he did in 1:1. Jesus was a very popular name in the first century and was the Greek form of the Hebrew name Joshua. In their gospels, Luke and Matthew make it clear that Joshua means 'God's salvation'; that is Jesus' role. However, for the most part Jesus is used in the gospels to refer to the historical, human person who suffered and died like any other human being. That is certainly the reaction of the town's people at Nazareth, who consider his only skill to be that of a carpenter.
- Jesus is referred to as the son of Mary (6:3). This was unusual as it was normal to refer to someone with reference to their father. It may be that Jesus' father, Joseph, is dead (the other gospels suggest that he married Mary when she was very young and he was an old man) or that they are being deliberately rude. It is unlikely that they are referring to the miraculous virgin birth of Jesus.
- The reference to his brothers and sisters simply stresses Jesus' ordinary human life. Some later Christian scholars suggested that brothers and sisters (6:5) should be translated as half-brothers and half-sisters to allow for Mary's virgin birth and perpetual virginity (i.e. that she had no further children after Jesus). But many modern interpreters consider that such an interpretation is reading too much into Mark's narrative.
- For Mark, Jesus' special relationship with God is demonstrated through his teaching, his wisdom and his miracles. It is a constant theme of Mark's Gospel that Jesus' authority to interpret the Torah is one which gives the people a real sense of its meaning and not one that is complicated by the complex rituals and rules of the Pharisees. So, the irony is that although they sense Jesus' supernatural powers, this quickly disappears when they just think of him as the young man from their town. That is why Jesus is unable to perform miracles (except for the few who had faith).

The Virgin Mary. Mary has an important place in Mark's Gospel, but did he think Jesus had a miraculous birth?

A New Approach – St Mark's Gospel

SON OF GOD

In the Old Testament the phrase **Son of God** could refer to God's angels (Genesis 6:2), to Israel (Hosea 11:1), to the king (2 Samuel 7:14), or to the righteous saints of Israel (Ecclesiasticus 4:10). In other words it did not refer to the messiah, but to those who had a very close relationship with God. But in the Roman world the emperors such as Caligula and Hadrian were called the sons of God in the same way as the Egyptian pharaohs were considered to be the descendants of the sun god Ra.

In Mark, the term Son of God is used in a very special way to express Jesus' unique relationship with God, which is closely linked with his sacrificial death and resurrection.

KEY QUESTION

Does the term 'Son of God' mean that Jesus was actually the same as God?

PERSPECTIVES

Jesus is either a lunatic or Son of God

The enormously popular and influential writer on Christianity C S Lewis (1898–1963) wrote the following about Jesus' divinity. He clearly rejects the liberal Christian view, but to what extent is his presentation of Jesus consistent with Mark's Gospel?

'I am trying here to prevent anyone saying the really foolish thing that people often say about Him; 'I'm ready to accept Jesus as a great moral teacher, but I don't accept His claim to be God'. That is one thing we must not say. A man who was merely a man and said the sort of things Jesus said would not be a great moral teacher. He would either be a lunatic – on a level with the man who says he is a poached egg – or else he would be the Devil of Hell. You must make your choice. Either this man was, and is, the Son of God: or else a madman or something worse.'

C S Lewis, *Mere Christianity*

Do you agree with C S Lewis that the choice is either that Jesus is the Son of God or was a madman?

C S Lewis

The baptism of Jesus (1:9–11)

The baptism of Jesus marks the moment when he becomes aware of his public role: to preach to Israel the message about the Kingdom of God as God's chosen one. Mark presents John the Baptist as the great prophet Elijah who, according to Malachi 4:5, would return to announce the coming of the messiah. This he does by calling the people to repentance and offering them the symbolism of a water baptism.

> See I will send you the prophet Elijah before the great and dreadful day of the LORD comes. He will turn the hearts of the fathers to their children and the hearts of the children to their fathers.
>
> *Malachi 4:5*

But Jesus' subsequent call to the people to repent (1:15) is no longer just a preparation for the coming of a future Kingdom but essential if the Kingdom is to become a present reality in our hearts.

- Jesus is called 'Son' by God not in the same way that the Roman emperors were called sons, but in the Old Testament sense of a person like the king or the righteous who were God's specially chosen 'sons'.

- The voice of God from heaven quotes part of Psalm 2, originally addressed to the king, 'You are my Son, today I have become your Father' (Psalm 2:7).

- But unlike the king's relationship with God, the quotation from Psalm 2 is altered to read 'You are my Son, whom I love' (1:11). By using 'love' Mark means that Jesus' relationship is unique; there can only be one Father–Son relationship.

- As God's Son, Jesus perhaps knows that this will mean being obedient to God as his Father, even if this means suffering and death. We can see this at the Garden of Gethsemane (14:36) when he addresses God as Abba or Father, knowing that his baptism would eventually lead to his death as a martyr. This is how he understood his baptism when he spoke to James and John about their future deaths as Christian martyrs, 'You will drink the cup I drink and be baptised with the baptism I am baptised with.' (10:39).

Read Unit 2, pages 20–21 for more about baptism in Christianity today.

The baptism of Jesus by John. Did Jesus know that this could lead to his eventual death?

Transfiguration (9:2–8)

KEY QUESTION

What is the purpose of the story of Jesus' transfiguration?

The Transfiguration is a strange incident in Mark's Gospel (John's Gospel does not include it). In many ways it is like the baptism of Jesus, only this time it is a private experience of the disciples when they come to see Jesus as the 'Son'. Despite this extraordinary insight, Mark makes it clear that none of the group of specially chosen disciples (Peter, James and John) understand the full meaning of this experience until after the resurrection. It is a difficult story and has many interpretations. Here are some:

- It is an insight into Jesus' divine nature as God's Son.
- It is a moment when the disciples understand Jesus' relationship with God and his place in Jewish history.
- It forms a spiritual baptism of the closest of Jesus' disciples (note how close the language is to Jesus' own baptism). The voice of God this time speaks to *them* and not to Jesus.

- It is a vision of Jesus' glorious resurrected state and is therefore a vision of future hope.
- It is a symbolic story about relationships in the Kingdom of God when it is completed. It will be a time when all the promises made in the Old Testament (represented by Moses as the Law and Elijah as the prophets) will be fulfilled because Jesus is God's Son.

The Transfiguration depends on a good knowledge of Old Testament ideas for its meaning.

- 'High mountain' (9:2) is a place of special religious significance. Moses, for example, came into the presence of God's glory whilst receiving the Law on Mount Sinai (Exodus 24:16).

> When Moses came down from Mount Sinai with the two tablets of the Testimony in his hands, he was not aware that his face was radiant because he had spoken with the Lord.
>
> *Exodus 34:29*

The Transfiguration. Why are Elijah and Moses depicted in such similar ways?

- Just as in Jesus' baptism, the 'cloud' (9:7) represents the presence of God. Moses also had been led by a cloudy pillar during the time of the exodus from Egypt (Exodus 13:2) and now the cloud represents God's presence in a moment of profound religious experience for Jesus and, especially, his disciples.

- The disciples experience Jesus' changed state by saying that 'His clothes became dazzling white' (9:3). Some people have described those who have been deep in prayer to be so spiritually transformed that their appearance has changed, just in the same way that Moses' face shone when he came into the presence of God (Exodus 34:29).

- In some Jewish writings, it was thought that Moses and Elijah (representing the Law and the prophets) would both have to return at the start of the age to come. But the vision (9:4) now suggests that the Kingdom of God will only be possible though Jesus as God's Son – as was prophesied in the Law and the prophets (i.e. the Old Testament).

- Why does Peter offer to build three shelters (9:5)? This is an odd part of the story. On the one hand he is so over-awed by the experience that in typical Peter fashion he appears to say whatever comes into his head. But on the other hand tents were built by the Israelites during the exodus. From early Jewish times, the people built shelters or tents during the festival of Sukkoth (or Tents) as a reminder of times when God was with them in the wilderness and helped them. So, the tent also symbolised the time when God would again reveal himself fully to the world in the age to come and when everyone would live in tents. So, when Peter asks whether he should build three shelters, he has sort of understood the religious meaning of the vision but perhaps his foolishness is that he thinks he needs *three* tents, when in fact they will *all* need tents. Mark doesn't make this entirely clear.

- God says to the disciples, 'This is my Son, whom I love. Listen to him.' (9:7). Previously at Caesarea Philippi, Peter had said that Jesus was the messiah although he could not accept that Jesus would have to suffer. Now he is being told that Jesus is the messiah, and he should understand and listen to Jesus' teaching that as God's Son he will have to suffer for others. This is why on their way down the mountain Jesus explains that their experience of him in his gloried state will make no sense until after the resurrection.

High Priest's Accusation (14:61)

We have seen (see Unit 7, page 86) the circumstances that led the High Priest to ask, 'Are you the Christ, the Son of the Blessed One?'. But what did the High Priest mean? 'Blessed One' was another way of referring to God without directly saying God's name, which would be blasphemous. So the High Priest is asking Jesus whether he is the messiah and the Son of God. Unusually, in Jewish theological terms, he has linked the idea of Son of God with messianic expectation. However, he probably did not mean that Jesus was divine but was questioning his claims of being God's chosen one acting on God's authority.

But, from the Christian point of view, Mark enjoys the irony that the Jewish High Priest has spoken the truth without being aware of it.

The Jewish festival of Sukkoth or Tents reminds the people of the presence of God.

Centurion's Comment (15:39)

> When the centurion, who stood there in front of Jesus, heard his cry and saw how he died, he said, 'Surely this man was the Son of God!'
>
> *Mark 15:39*

Significantly, it is a Gentile, a Roman Centurion who, impressed with Jesus' death, finally sees Jesus not as a prophet, Elijah or a Davidic messiah but as 'the Son of God'. It is possible that as a non-Jew he sees Jesus as one of the great Roman or Greek heroes of the past who had been called 'son of God' or **saviour**. But the point Mark is making is that for Christians, Jesus is Son because of his extraordinary relationship with God, especially in death.

Read also Unit 7, page 90.

A Roman centurion

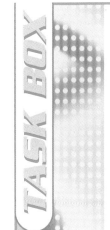

TASK BOX

a) Draw the Transfiguration as a picture or diagram.

b) Explain the purpose of Moses, Elijah and Peter in Jesus' Transfiguration.

c) Discuss the following statement by a liberal Christian: 'When Christians say that Jesus was the Son of God, they mean he was specially inspired by God.'

TEST YOURSELF

1 Give two meanings of the term Son of God in the Old Testament.

2 What did God's voice say to Jesus at his baptism?

3 How did Jesus appear at the Transfiguration?

4 Who appeared with Jesus at the Transfiguration?

5 What did God say to the disciples at the Transfiguration?

6 Which two Old Testament people appeared at the Transfiguration?

7 Why does Peter think he should build three shelters or tents at the Transfiguration?

8 What question did the High Priest ask Jesus about his identity at his trial?

9 What did the centurion say when he saw how Jesus died?

SON OF MAN

KEY QUESTION

Why did Jesus use the unusual term Son of Man to refer to himself and not the title Son of God or messiah?

The phrase **Son of Man** is only used by Jesus of himself. It is a strange term and no one is quite sure why Jesus should have chosen it or exactly what he meant by it. He appears to use it in three ways to mean that:

- as Son of Man he is to be an example to others of one who carries out God's will
- as Son of Man he is a representative of human suffering for others
- as Son of Man he is God's judge on earth and in heaven.

In other words, Jesus used the title because it was intentionally ambiguous and included many of the various messianic hopes at the time in a special way.

Caesarea Philippi (8:27–37)

Jesus has travelled north towards the Syrian boundary into an area that one of Herod's sons, Philip, had dedicated to the Roman Emperor. In the synoptic gospels this incident marks the turning point of Jesus' ministry and the first of three predictions about his suffering as the Son of Man. Jesus uses the term to clarify what Peter had said when he called Jesus the messiah. But it is clear that Peter had not expected the messiah to suffer and he tells Jesus off. Jesus reacts very strongly and accuses Peter of being possessed by Satan. The role of the Son of Man is not to achieve political or earthly power, but has a much more complex mission to bring humans into a new relationship with God. In the rest of the story (8:34–37) Jesus' teaching is about following the example of the Son of Man, even if this leads to death (see Unit 5, page 54).

The traditional site of Caesarea Philippi. Why is this the turning point in Jesus' ministry?

> Peter answered, 'You are the Christ.' ... He began to teach them that the Son of Man must suffer many things and be rejected by the elders, chief priests and teachers of the law and that he must be killed and after three days rise again.

Mark 8:29–31

The Son of Man will be ashamed of him when he comes in his Father's glory with the holy angels.

Mark 8:37

There are three ways in which the term 'Son of Man' is used:

- The phrase Son of Man simply means 'I' or 'me'. Jesus perhaps meant that his life is a model or example of how humans are to behave. Jesus says the person who wishes to be his disciple and follow the example of the Son of Man must 'deny himself and take up his cross and follow me' (8:34).

- Son of Man indicates Jesus' suffering role as a martyr and representative of others. Jesus, and certainly the gospel writers, could see that his life mirrored the life of the Suffering Servant in the prophecy of Isaiah (52:13–53:12) whose death enabled those who had persecuted him to have their sins forgiven. That is certainly what Jesus had in mind when, after telling off James and John for their misunderstanding of the Kingdom as a political kingdom, he taught them that if they are to be true followers they must be prepared to suffer for others. The Kingdom can only become a reality if humans are generous and make sacrifices for others. This is why Jesus said, 'The Son of Man did not come to be served, but to serve, and to give his life as a ransom for many' (10:45).

- The Son of Man is also used by Jesus to mean one who has God's authority to judge. For example, when Jesus cures the Paralysed Man he says he is acting as the Son of Man with God's authority to forgive the man's sins on earth (2:10). Other passages suggest that Jesus also appears to have imagined that he would be like the heavenly figure in Daniel 7:13, the one 'like the son of man' sent by God to judge the world. These sayings refer to the time when the Son of Man would be resurrected and seen in glory to judge the world and choose the elect (13:26). This is how he describes his role as the Son of Man to the High Priest at his trial (14:62) and how he concludes his teaching at Caesarea Philippi when he warns those who have failed to live the life of humility (8:38).

THE MESSIAH AND THE SON OF DAVID

KEY QUESTION

Did Jesus sometimes think of himself as a political messiah?

In response to Jesus' question at Caesarea Philippi: 'Who do people say I am?' (8:27) various responses indicate the popular recognition of Jesus as either being a prophet, or Elijah (or his reincarnation) or John the Baptist (perhaps they believed John's spirit had entered into Jesus after he had been executed by Herod Antipas). Jesus then asked them what they had been telling the crowds. Peter, as spokesman for the disciples and as the future leader of the Church, said: 'You are the Christ' (8:29).

In the Old Testament, 'messiah' (or 'Christ' in its Greek form) simply meant the 'anointed one' and often referred to the king who was anointed with oil at his enthronement. There had gradually built up an idea based on passages such as 2 Samuel 7 (see previous page), that the messiah would be a descendent of the great King David and like him would establish a new kingdom in which God and Israel would live in harmony for ever. The title certainly had strongly political elements because the messiah's role would be to throw out Israel's enemies.

> I will raise up your offspring to succeed you, who will come from your own body, and I will establish his Kingdom. He is the one who will build a house for my Name, and I will establish the throne of his Kingdom for ever.

2 Samuel 7:12–13

God's words to King David looking forward to the messiah.

Some thought a descendant of King David would be a warrior messiah.

But there are several reasons why the Davidic messiah-type appears to have been greatly modified by Jesus.

- Jesus' understanding of his role as messiah involves suffering (8:31), which, as we have seen, Peter finds very difficult to accept.
- Even though at the Triumphal entry (11:4–11) the crowd hail him as the messiah who is bringing in the Davidic kingdom (11:10), Jesus rides a colt into Jerusalem as a sign of peace (Read Unit 6, pages 69–70).

- Only blind Bartimaeus calls Jesus the Son of David (10:47), for although he is blind he is spiritually able to see Jesus as the messiah who brings mercy and healing.
- Finally, in a complicated passage (12:35–37), Mark records a conversation between Jesus and the crowd in which he argues that he is the Son of David. However this is not to be understood literally, because if David says in Psalm 110 that the messiah is his 'Lord', then he must be spiritually superior to him and cannot therefore biologically be his son.

TASK BOX

Could Jesus have been a political revolutionary?

a) Consider the following statements (make sure you look up the passages referred to).

In each case state whether you think the statement is true or false. Give a brief reason for each decision.

- Jesus thought he was a military messiah because at the feeding of the 5000 he sat the people in ranks of fifties and hundreds as if he were organising an army (6:40) and led them.
- Jesus thought he was a military messiah because amongst his disciples two were nicknamed the 'Sons of Thunder' and Simon was a Zealot freedom fighter (3:13–19).
- Judas betrayed Jesus because he thought Jesus was going to be a political leader (14:10–11).
- Jesus was popular with the ordinary people because he was leading a political revolution (2:17).
- Jesus' triumphal entry into Jerusalem and cleansing of the Temple were signs that he wanted a religious and political revolution (11:1–19).
- Pilate was right to consider Jesus as a political threat to Rome as 'King of the Jews' (15:2).

b) Find out about Camilo Torres. Describe his fight for freedom in Latin America. Was it right for him, as a Christian priest, to be a soldier in a political revolutionary movement?

A New Approach – St Mark's Gospel

1 Give an example of Jesus as Son of Man who has the authority to forgive sins.
2 Give a saying of Jesus which shows that the Son of Man is one who suffers as an example to others.
3 Give a saying of Jesus which shows that as Son of Man he will be God's judge of the world.
4 Describe what kind of messiah the Jews hoped for in Jesus' time.
5 What did blind Bartimaeus shout out when he heard that Jesus had arrived in Jericho?
6 Which of Jesus' disciples might have been linked to a political movement?
7 Give one indication that Jesus was not a military messiah.

SAVIOUR

For fundamentalist and conservative Christians in particular, Jesus' miracles are significant in demonstrating his divinity and role as saviour. Unlike miracle workers in the Old Testament, as well as the disciples themselves and faith healers today, where God is thought to be working through the person, Jesus performs his own miracles because he is God. Jesus performed nature miracles in which he dealt with inanimate things (such as storms and food) and healing miracles that directly involved people.

The term saviour is not used in Mark, but every miracle shows how, when Jesus heals a person or restores nature, he also removes sins and establishes the Kingdom of God. That is why the word saviour is appropriate because in Greek it means 'to heal' as well as 'to save' from sin.

We know that this man really is Saviour of the world.

John 4:42

There are very few references to Jesus as 'Saviour' in the gospels, although it became a very popular title later in early Christianity.

Every healing miracle in Mark should therefore be interpreted on two levels:

■ the physical (the cure)
■ the spiritual (as a moment of salvation when sin is removed).

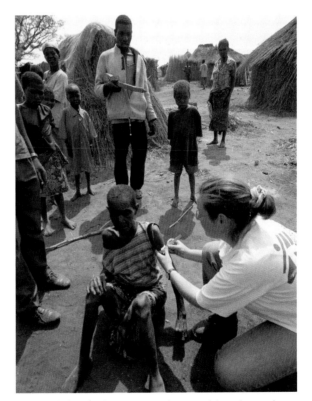

In Jesus' time a doctor was also considered a saviour. Healing the body was a way of curing the soul.

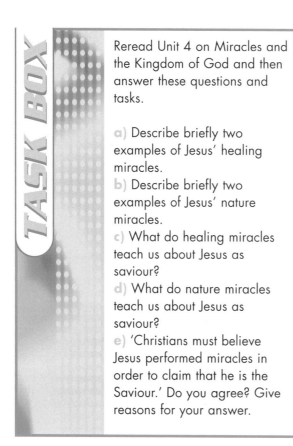

TASK BOX

Reread Unit 4 on Miracles and the Kingdom of God and then answer these questions and tasks.

a) Describe briefly two examples of Jesus' healing miracles.

b) Describe briefly two examples of Jesus' nature miracles.

c) What do healing miracles teach us about Jesus as saviour?

d) What do nature miracles teach us about Jesus as saviour?

e) 'Christians must believe Jesus performed miracles in order to claim that he is the Saviour.' Do you agree? Give reasons for your answer.

How do we treat those whom we think are mad?

Here are two more healing miracles that have not been discussed in earlier units and that both present Jesus as saviour.

The Madman at the Tombs (5:1–10)

This story is also known as the Healing of Legion, or the Healing of Mob, or the Gerasene demoniac, because the man whom Jesus cures is possessed by a vast number of evil spirits. When Jesus asks the man his name, he gives him his nickname, 'My name is Legion, for we are many' (5:9). A legion in the Roman army was a unit of 6000 men. This story is therefore a spectacular cure and plays an especially important part in Mark's presentation of Jesus as the one who not only cures a man who is mentally very ill and rejected by society (he lives outside the village in the local burial ground), but also defeats Satan's army of demons in the establishment of the Kingdom of God.

■ Mark goes to great lengths to give a very full description of the events. Legion's mental illness is so bad that it has given him superhuman strength. Whenever the locals tie him up, he simply snaps his chains. He cuts himself with stones and howls day and night.

■ Legion lives amongst the tombs probably because they were considered unclean. So for the locals this howling and bloody man just reinforced their fears that he was indeed possessed by Satan's army of evil spirits.

■ Legion is just like the Strongman Jesus spoke about in his parable (3:27). In the parable the Strongman represented Satan and his kingdom, so it is not surprising then that as Jesus approaches Legion, the evil spirits shout out Jesus' true identity, 'Jesus, Son of the Most High God' (5:7). 'The Most High God' was a term that Gentiles often used to refer to the Jewish God and, as Jesus is in Gentile territory (the area known as Decapolis) as in other exorcisms, evil recognises Jesus as God's agent, and even worships him (5:6), whereas ordinary humans often do not.

- Jesus asks the spirits their name (5:9) as the standard means of carrying out an exorcism. It was thought that once the evil spirit could be named, then it could be summoned out of the person. Some interpreters of this passage comment that Jesus' power is so strong that the spirits give him their name immediately, whilst others think that they are trying to fool Jesus by giving him the man's nickname. Jesus ignores this and carries out the exorcism anyway.
- In other stories of exorcisms at the time, it was quite standard for demons to beg not to be sent 'out of the area' (5:10). Jesus allows them their request to enter into a herd of pigs. From the Jewish point of view this would have been quite understandable as pigs were considered unclean. But the twist in the story is yet to come. The spirits might have thought that they had tricked Jesus into allowing them to continue to exist, but the pigs rushed down the steep bank into the lake and were drowned (5:13).
- So evil is destroyed and Jesus' authority as God's saviour is established. This is shown by the fact that the man is completely spiritually and physically cured (5:15). The man wants to become a disciple, but Jesus sends him to preach in the Decapolis or Ten Town area on the west of the river Jordan, an area that was primarily occupied by Gentiles. The Kingdom is seen to spread abroad, overcoming evil and superstition, which may also be a reason why Mark so likes the story as this was similar to the situation in Rome in the years between 60–70 CE.
- Some people think that Jesus' destruction of the pigs was immoral because he has deprived the locals of their livelihood and that is why they wanted Jesus to leave (5:17). This could be so, but it is more likely that they were just as frightened by Jesus' supernatural powers as by Legion's behaviour and they wanted to be left in peace. Their superstitious reaction is in contrast to Legion's faith.

[Look again at Unit 1, pages 13–14 at the way different Christians interpret this story.]

Healing the Deaf and Dumb Man (7:31–37)

This story forms part of Mark's narrative (7:24–8:12) when Jesus is presented as saviour to the Gentiles. The Healing of the Deaf Man is especially important because, unlike the story of Legion, the Gentile people in Decapolis are amazed by his authority and say, 'He has done everything well' (7:37).

Because the man is deaf he can only mumble words (7:32). It is the *people's* faith, just like the faith of the Paralysed Man's friends (2:1–11), rather than the faith of the man himself that enables Jesus to cure him. He treats the man in a way that they would all have recognised as the usual method of the local medicine men. Jesus put his fingers in the man's ears and spits on his tongue, sighs and says the 'magic' word 'Ephphatha'.

But the importance of the story for Mark is that Jesus is the saviour who makes the ears of the deaf 'unstopped' and 'the mute tongue shout for joy' in the fulfilment of Isaiah's prophecy (Isaiah 35:5–6) of the age to come. Mark even presents the Gentile people as knowing the prophecy because they quote it at the end of the story (7:37).

This is quite a contrast to Jesus' own disciples who, although they 'see' and 'hear' Jesus frequently, fail to understand who Jesus is or to live up to his teaching. Look again at Unit 5, pages 56–57.

THE 'MESSIANIC SECRET'

KEY QUESTION

Did Jesus want to keep his true identity a secret during his lifetime?

There are many occasions when Jesus tells people not to say who he is. This has caused some scholars to call this Mark's '**messianic secret**'. But is there really a secret and if so why does Jesus demand it? Here are some suggestions:

- Jesus' identity comes only with proper considered insight. The command to silence is so that the reader should think for him or herself what it means to say that Jesus is the Son of God.
- The claim to be 'Son of God' could easily be misunderstood by others. It could be confused to mean that Jesus was some kind of wonder worker or magician or military messiah. The command was to stop the crowds getting the wrong idea about Jesus' identity.
- The full meaning of Jesus' identity can only be understood after his crucifixion and resurrection. As both of these happen after Jesus' call to secrecy, Jesus wanted his followers to believe only in him after he had risen. So, for example, the centurion says at the moment of Jesus' death, 'Surely this man was Son of God' (15:39).
- The 'secret' was invented by Mark to explain why Jesus never claimed during his lifetime to be the Son of God. Because the early Christians did think Jesus was the Son of God, his embarrassing silence was therefore considered to be part of Jesus' original intention during his ministry.
- The 'secret' was Mark's way of explaining why so many failed to recognise Jesus as the long-awaited messiah.

TASK BOX

- He would not let the demons speak, because they knew who he was. (1:34)
- 'See that you don't tell this to anyone. But go, show your self to the priest ...' (1:44)
- And he gave them strict orders not to let anyone know about this, and told them to give her something to eat. (5:43)
- Jesus commanded them not to tell anyone. But the more he did so the more they kept talking about it. (7:36)
- Jesus warned them not to tell anyone about him. (8:30)
- As they were coming down the mountain, Jesus gave them orders not to tell anyone what they had seen, until the Son of Man had risen from the dead. (9:9)

a) Read the quotations above and briefly describe in each case the situation where Jesus called for silence about his identity.
b) Explain why Jesus may have called for secrecy about his identity.
c) Look up the following references in Mark, 1:28, 2:12, 3:20–30, 5:19, 6:54, and explain what these passages tell you about knowledge of Jesus' identity.
d) Discuss both sides of the debate: 'Mark does not have a messianic secret.'

TEST YOURSELF

1. Give two meanings of the word 'saviour'.
2. Why was the madman at the tombs called Legion?
3. How did Jesus cure Legion of his evil spirits?
4. What did Jesus tell Legion to do after his cure?
5. What was the special word Jesus used in his cure of the deaf and dumb man?
6. Which prophecy in the Old Testament did the cure of the deaf and dumb man fulfil?
7. Give two examples of Jesus commanding silence after a healing.
8. Give two reasons why scholars think Mark has a 'messianic secret'.
9. Give one reason why scholars think Mark does not have a 'messianic secret'.

1
  a. Who was Legion? [2]
  b. Outline the events at Caesarea Philippi. [6]
  c. Explain why Mark uses the title messiah (Christ) to describe Jesus. [8]
  d. 'Jesus was a good man, nothing more.'
     Do you agree? Give reasons for your opinion, showing you have considered another
     point of view. In your answer you should refer to Mark's Gospel. [4]

2
  a. Describe the Transfiguration of Jesus. [8]
  b. Explain why the story of the Transfiguration is important to Christians. [7]
  c. 'Mark's gospel shows Jesus to be a very different kind of leader (messiah) from the one
     the Jews expected.'
     Do you agree? Give reasons to support your answer and show that you have thought about
     different points of view. [5]

Assignment

WEBLINKS

- More about C S Lewis:
  http://members.aol.com/
  thompsonja/cslewis.htm
- Camilo Torres, priest and
  soldier:
  http://www.greenleft.org.au/
  back/1996/219/219p16.htm
- Jesus and what people
  think about him:
  www.whoisjesus-really.com/
  english/default.htm
- On the 'messianic secret'
  in Mark: http://people.smu.edu/
  dwatson/messianic_secret_001.htm
- Pictures of Jesus, his life and
  influence: www.rejesus.co.uk/
  expressions/faces_jesus/index.html
- As Son of God:
  www.bbc.co.uk/religion/programmes/sog

REMEMBER

- Mark considers Jesus to be a mysterious and enigmatic figure.
- Jesus never explicitly claims to be Son of God; he refers to himself as Son of Man.
- Jesus' miracles were central to revealing his role as saviour.
- Jesus' death and resurrection are essential to the understanding of his role as messiah.

Key Words

age to come In Jewish thought many of the prophets looked forward to a time when God would remove all suffering and injustice. They contrasted the age to come with the present age, the times in which we still live.

allegory parable A complex type of parable, told by Jesus, where each part of the story symbolises an important idea.

Apostles Jesus chose some of his closest disciples (the 12) to continue his teaching and be an example after his death (Judas was replaced by Matthias). An apostle means literally 'one who is sent' and has also come to refer to anyone who has brought Christianity to a country.

baptism The moment when, for many Christians, a person becomes a member of the Christian church (or worldwide community of Christians).

blasphemy Any act that challenges the supremacy of God. In Jewish law this could mean challenging the place of the Temple or setting one's self up to be equal with God. The High Priest charged Jesus with committing blasphemy.

Christ/messiah The two terms from the Greek and Hebrew words meaning 'anointed one'. They quickly came to describe Jesus' special relationship with God. Originally, Messiah referred to a military figure such as King David.

Church This can be used in two senses. The Church refers to all Christians throughout the world. A church is a building where people worship. It is used mostly in its first meaning throughout this book.

Conservatives Those who believe that the Bible is true but may contain human interpretations.

disciple Anyone who follows the example and teaching of Jesus.

eschatology The technical word used to mean discussion of the future when God will establish a new and perfect world.

exorcism A special form of healing when an evil spirit is expelled from a person (or place).

eyewitnesses Those who saw and heard what Jesus did and said.

Fundamentalist, Conservative and Liberal Different modern Christian interpretations of miracles.

Fundamentalists Those who consider that the Bible is God's Word and therefore cannot be in error.

Gentiles People who are not Jewish. There was much debate amongst Jewish scholars about whether Gentiles would be included in the age to come.

Gospel The good news that Jesus is God's Son.

healing miracle A moment when a person's illness is removed by Jesus as God's Son and they feel restored. In Mark these are also symbols of the Kingdom of God.

judgement Before the Kingdom of God can be established, God judges everyone on the goodness of their moral and spiritual lives.

Liberals Those who believe that the Bible is written by humans in their own words.

Literalists Those who consider every word of the Bible is God-given.

messianic secret The term used by scholars to refer to the several occasions when Jesus commanded people or evil spirits to be silent about his identity.

miracle A moment when God acts in a powerful and special way in the world.

nature miracles A special moment when Jesus as God's Son alters the laws of nature for human advantage.

New Testament The second part of the Christian Bible, which proclaims that Jesus is the Son of God.

Old Testament The Jewish Hebrew Bible and for Christians the preparation for the New Testament.

oral law The oral interpretation of the written law of Moses (the Torah), which the Pharisees followed because they thought it would make them holy.

parable A story or saying that uses an event from everyday life to explain something about the Kingdom of God. Jesus used different kinds of parable depending on the situation.

Passion story The story of Jesus' suffering or 'passion', from his anointing at Bethany until his crucifixion.

Passover One of the three great pilgrim festivals in Judaism, which celebrates the time when the Jews were freed from slavery in Egypt and journeyed to the Promised Land.

Pharisees Those who were not priests but who believed that by keeping to the oral law they would receive reward in the afterlife.

praxis This term means 'faith in action'. Feeding the poor and upholding justice in society are two examples of Christian praxis.

priests Those who, through birth, assisted in the Temple in Jerusalem. The senior priests or 'chief priests' assisted the High Priest.

repentance Repentance is more than just saying sorry; it is a change of heart and mind leading to a new way of life.

resurrection The moment when, in Christian thought, the body is transformed after death and the soul and new body live on in the afterlife. This is *not* the same as reincarnation (when the soul is given a new body).

riddle parable Parables designed to intrigue and challenge.

Sadducees These came largely from senior Jerusalem priestly families. They did not believe in the oral law or life after death.

Sanhedrin or the Great Assembly This was the senior law court in Israel, made up of 71 members. It comprised chief priests, senior members of society and scribes (or lawyers). They condemned Jesus to death for blasphemy.

Saviour 'One who saves' or 'heals'. The title is not used in Mark but it is implied by all Jesus' miracles when he heals, forgives, provides and rescues.

sayings parable Parables designed to be easily memorable by being catchy and short.

Son of God In the Old Testament this referred either to the King or to Israel or to a righteous person. The gospels use it to refer to Jesus' special relationship with God. The title is never used by Jesus.

Son of Man A difficult title to interpret. It is only used by Jesus to describe his role as 'man for others', a suffering servant and God's chosen one who would judge on earth and in heaven.

teachers of the law or scribes These were Israel's civil servants. Many assisted in the Temple law court.

Torah or written law This was given to Moses at Mount Sinai and contained 613 commandments covering every aspect of life. Found in the first books of the Old Testament or Hebrew Bible.

tradition Another term used by Mark to refer to the oral law, or the customs of worship passed by the Pharisees but not ones necessarily found in the Torah.

treason Any act that undermines the authority of the government. Pontius Pilate found Jesus guilty of being a threat to the authority of Roman rule. The punishment was death.

vocation Means that someone feels that they are being called by God to carry out a particular task or job.

Word of God The way in which God expresses himself to humans.

word-of-mouth Describes the stories and sayings of Jesus as they were passed on orally.

Index